D1300121

8/17/21

one
headlight

Taco
Sam
Thanks
you.

[see ch 12]

a memoir

matt caprioli

CIRQUE PRESS

CIRQUE PRESS

Sandra Kleven — Michael Burwell
3157 Bettles Bay Loop,
Anchorage, AK 99515

cirquejournal@gmail.com
www.cirquejournal.com

Cover and book design by Emily Tallman, Poetica
Author photo by Emil D. Cohen

Print ISBN: 978-1-7375104-4-4

for Abigail Ruth Frye

Today,
at her age, I was driving myself home from yet
another spine appointment, singing along
to some maudlin but solid song on the radio,
and I saw a mom take her raincoat off
and give it to her young daughter when
a storm took over the afternoon. My god,
I thought, my whole life I've been under her
raincoat thinking it was somehow a marvel
that I never got wet.

—Ada Limón, "The Raincoat"

CONTENTS

Part One

CHAPTER 1

Storm

We didn't care that the weather was unkind. Walking from baggage claim, she asked me all excited, "You want to get some hot cocoa from Denny's?"

She was 39. I was 12.

"Sure. Let's do it."

Pubescent boys shouldn't be so thrilled at seeing their mother. That's why my eyes twitched around the airport with all those people around. They leaned over railings, eager for a glimpse of their loved one. I kept my neck bent at 45 degrees. I was embarrassed to lock eyes with a stranger and risk entry into the crossfire of their intimacy, watch their face dim then slacken at the appearance of little ole me. If Mom suffered similar hesitations in public, she never showed them. Or perhaps I never noticed. She found a level of giddiness, which I suppose is pure joy, that I was too anxious to embrace. She went wild as soon as I entered her line of vision — nuts, in fact: jumping up and down, waving and shouting:

"Matthew! I see you! I see you! *iiiIIII* see you!"

She calmed herself to step back and take a photo of me walking past security, the first of 24 shots on a bulky disposable camera. With some disappointment, I see these photos now to find that I dropped my face in each one. I am a pudgy brat boy, bowl haircut, too terrorized by my own realities to love others. The pictures don't capture just how sensitive and paranoid I was against judgment. I told Mom to stop acting so excited at the airport. People looking at her embarrassed me; her antics increased the chance that they might look at me.

And how may have people viewed her? In a photo from 2002, she's in a long blue snow coat with black shoulder pads and a bright red turtleneck underneath — a gilt necklace above her heart, her favorite piece of jewelry, in the shape of a cross. She's making her way through three feet of snow on top of a mountain, smiling brilliantly with absolute happiness. Her face is kind, beautiful in clean symmetry, and her bangs remain buoyant from the Sunday service. Her most remarkable feature is her smile. Everyone knew Abby for her smile. I retain few photos and memories where she is not smiling.

I didn't let myself be tightly hugged till we were in the beat-down Mustang, safe from the snow in the parking garage. The Mustang was built to be deep cobalt, but several decades of driving around Alaska had clawed the hot ride into a frayed, wiry mess, so that the exterior cut anyone foolish enough to coast their fingertips along the hood. Mom had been driving all winter without a passenger window. For the past year, she had been saying the gap would be fixed by the time of my visit (she'd keep driving like that for two more winters before she scrounged up the money for a replacement window). She also cheerfully informed me that the right headlight was "feeling sick" and was scheduled to be fixed next week. This is all to say that nearing midnight on March 16, 2002, on what would become known as The Saint Patrick's Day Storm, we drove into the worst snowstorm in the history of Anchorage in a rickety old Mustang with no passenger window and one headlight.

Snow belly-flopped on the Mustang's roof as soon as we left the parking garage. "Oh right then, Matthew," my mother said brightly. "On second thought, maybe we should just head straight to The Valley."

The Valley was the Matanuska-Susitna Valley, specifically the edge of it, Lazy Mountain, where my grandmother lived near the top in a slipshod, two-story cabin. The thick brush and weeds made a dense fence around the acre of arid land, as high as three feet in the summer; in the winter, snow packed upon itself even higher. From the dirt driveway, you walked up dogwood steps (Victoria, my grandmother, once stepped on a craggy upturned nail — went straight through her foot) and into the first kitchen, which was stacked with moldy smelling crates of bibles, photo negatives, and Barbie dolls. You passed the cardboard-thin stairs into the living room, which Victoria heated with an open furnace, fed by old newspapers and phone books. If you turned back, you saw the underside of the stairs, a cross-section revealing each hollow step. There were no enclosed ceilings, so puffs of yellow insulation bloomed through spindly rafters.

But I liked being up there with Mom. Her smiles and laughter, Grandma's erratic singing and claps to God; it all made the place feel warm, even when below zero. Victoria painted the walls in bright reds and yellows, which reminded her of her childhood home in Cottonwood, Arizona. Even if we had to wear snow pants for pajamas, we were happy.

My first night there a couple years back, Mom and I zipped ourselves up tight in sleeping bags on the kitchen floor, not only because we kept shivering, but also because Victoria had explained in her high-pitched chipper that the rustling, sandpapery noise we heard from the walls was *the shredders*.

"Don't worry *mijo*," she told me. "They don't want to eat you. They want Raisin Bran."

The snow was 8-10 inches deep when we left the airport. The Mustang handled well as International Airport Road morphed into Dimond Boulevard, named not after the jewel, but Anthony J. Dimond, an Alaskan territory rep who had overlapped with FDR and led the dissent to the Jewish state being set up in Alaska after WW2. I attended the school named after Representative A.J. Dimond, a squat grey building, where I was repeatedly shocked to discover who I was.

Mom reached the first red light on Dimond Boulevard and Old Seward, coincidentally near a Denny's, which was dark inside. It's a foul omen when a 24-hour Denny's closes, and perhaps it's then that I realized the major thoroughfare of Dimond Boulevard and The Dimond Center — "Alaska's Biggest Mall!!" — were entirely deserted, save for a few snowed-in vans and trucks. Streetlights benched inches of snow on their feeble-looking heads. I wondered if they could hurt themselves from carrying all that snow.

The light turned green. The Mustang couldn't move. It rocked in its self-made ruts, the front wheels charging forward, rocking back, trying and failing, like a person clawing for a lifesaver just out of reach. I sensed a panic in Mom's bright demeanor, or maybe it was the vision of us trapped by mounds of lead snow in a car that was hardly a foot above pavement on a good day. I pictured our skeletal bodies discovered in the summer. My mind leans frantic; even then, I zoomed to the worst-case scenario. But Mom, a former Marine, gripped the fluffy blue steering wheel and timed her body to roll with the car.

"Rock with me," she instructed, "Let's get Rocky out of here." (Rocky was her name for the Mustang; also the name of her favorite movie franchise; she wanted to name my half-sister Rocky until my dad said hell no). We rocked back and forth for a good minute. Eventually, our momentum swung together to shoot us out up onto the road.

"WaHoooo!" Mom yipped cowboy-style. Perhaps sensing my fear that certain death still surrounded us, she turned practical.

"Let's pray we get no more red lights."

The Lord granted our wishes (we ignored those two yellow-mostly-red lights) and the Mustang took us up the high, spiral ramp to the Glenn Highway, the only route that could carry us inland to The Valley.

Thus elevated, it became indisputably clear that we were at the center of a colossal storm. Wind hurled through our broken window. The howls sheathed us in a frigid vicing grip. The Mustang suddenly felt controlled by larger forces, as if the squalls were pulling us along on a string. The onslaught of snow erased the sparse streetlights strung along the vast highway. Our one functioning headlight let us see four feet in front.

Mom shook her head, chastising herself for not fixing the other headlight. "But every time I fix it, it just breaks down again the next week."

The right headlight did seem fated to break regularly. Mom tried to do most of her errands in the daylight so nobody would flash our "one-eyed bandit." When Mom did pay to fix the faulty headlight, it usually came back casting a greenish light or a glaring white beam that caused others to honk at us madly, shaking their heads at the assholes with their brights on. State troopers pulled us over, and she'd talk them into giving us more time.

"I found Petco of all places can do replacements for $13.25," she'd say in her sweetest voice. "I'm just waiting for my next check."

8

Mom sat at the edge of the driver's seat. She drove us at 20 mph.

"Matthew, why don't you put on some music," she said, calm and upbeat. "Anything you want."

I knew she was tired from two shifts in a bakery at The Dimond Center. A decade later, she'd admit she was too excited to see me and that sleep was impossible. This meant we were driving in the worst snowstorm Anchorage had ever seen in a rickety Mustang with one headlight and a driver who hadn't slept in nearly 42 hours.

It should be said that the Mustang had a temporary window: a provisional solution I devised the summer before where I hooked an old Lion King comforter to the passenger visor, pinned another corner to the "Jesus handle" in the rear, and bound the bottom tips with a couple of Grandma's old phone books. Mom called me a genius. It was enough to keep the snow from sidewinding into the car, but the cavernous wind still seeped in.

In the Mustang, I also learned that a sticky detachable remote-thing at the center console was, when properly connected and wiggled just right, the portal to a CD player. For us, a CD player in a car was the height of luxury; it was unexpected in a car the church had gifted out of pity. Since I discovered the hidden marvel, Abby always let me choose which album to play, even when my older sister, Lee Ann, joined us for a visit.

Against the storm, an EP from Faith Hill seemed appropriate. It featured remixes of "This Kiss." I had used all my allowance in California to buy it and pay for postage to Alaska without (of course) telling Dad. And for the many months where I was out of sight, she'd play the cheerful bops of Faith Hill.

"Whenever I missed you, I'd play her," she'd tell me once I became an adult. "That album helped me get through you being so far away."

By the fourth remix, she started nodding off. Her head jutted down and I yelled *Mom*. She perked up, her elbows shot straight. "Yes yes I'm awake!" She turned my way, smiling broadly. "Maybe we can play a game?" she asked.

We settled on singing gospel music. The music came from an Apostolic church we called Sylmar, after the suburban residential block it assumed in a Los Angeles neighborhood. I was baptized there at eight in a horse trough.

My father, a former altar boy, repeated his dismay in the waning weeks to the ceremony. "Are you freaking kidding me?" his booming voice moaned in the kitchen. Then the living room. The whole drive there. "This has got to be a joke." But he was wrong. I knew it then. Not only was religion no laughing matter, but it didn't matter where I was baptized so long as my heart was right with God. He was wrong, my father. As with so many things, I didn't think the horse trough was peculiar, and I sided with Abigail. Later on, I knew it was more complicated. They both were right and wrong at once.

Past Thunderbird Falls, Mom nodded off again. This time I poked her with the plastic tip of a pen.

"Ouch!"

"You have to stay awake," I whined.

She glanced at me, redoubled her focus on the road, and sat taller. "You got it co-captain."

To see her through the rest of the trip, I turned off the heat. The Mustang instantly lost all of its warmth, and our teeth began to chatter. But I knew how we could keep warm: Darlene Zschech, our favorite gospel singer. I forget if I skipped to the songs we unanimously agreed were the best: Shout to the Lord, My Redeemer Lives, Jesus Lover of My Soul. Looking back, it's easy to scoff at Darlene and her congregations. I stopped following her in 2004. I was in the closet and knew that under the teachings of my fundamentalist church, I had to follow God or Cock. As the former may not exist, I chose to embrace the more tangible reality of male genitalia. At 29, nearly a lifetime doubled, I'm quite distant from the teenager who wept at Bible camp, and distributed tracts on Acts 2:38 in Walmart parking lots.

Now, I'm amused to watch my memory of Darlene warp and distort through Facebook. When I was a major fan, I'm not sure she had a website. Now on Facebook, she has over a million likes, the banner page is a 20-second recursive clip of Darlene leading mass prayers, concerts where thousands jump up and down to her pacing around the stage. I watch this all on mute. I see the word *platform*. There she is making young people laugh. I sense this is some *platform* to engage "the youth." I step away from the computer for a glass of wine. "A *platform*" I say to myself incredulous. "She has a *platform* now."

But Darlene was necessary for us then, especially Mom. I see now via Wikipedia that Darlene had a miscarriage at 12 weeks in 2000, the same year Abby *lost her baby*, as she phrased it in a journal, at 25 weeks. The loss was so heartrending for Abby that she left my father and moved to Alaska to be near her own mother. I imagine Mom would have felt even greater camaraderie with Darlene had she known their shared trauma.

The music gave Mom a second lease on life. We had a "revival" in the car, clapping our hands, singing with Darlene, shouting when the chorus hit. Her eyes, as they always did in church, blazed with life, even as black gales kept shaking Rocky.

"We're gonna make it," she said as much to herself as me. "We're gonna make it."

We made it to Palmer. As in Anchorage, we were the only moving car. We drove through Downtown Palmer, the public showers, the shady VHS rental stores I'd come to know, then up to the mountain.

The main road up Lazy Mountain was full of peaks and valleys. The Mustang climbed the mountain slowly, without major issue, not even when the road turned to gravel. Luckily, no trees had fallen onto the winding roads, so Mom never had to slow our momentum. We made it more than halfway once the real challenge began.

Rounding a dark meadow, Mom drove "Rocky" through a field that in the summer was emerald and infinite. Once the meadow stopped, we were to drop 500 steep feet, then go up a sharper incline a good 300 feet taller. This also happened to be the point where the city of Palmer stopped all attempts at road maintenance, and the gravel abruptly transformed to jagged dirt and stone. Any plowing was done by residents who could afford Ford 350s.

"All right Matthew," Mom said. We couldn't avoid this moment any longer. "I'm going to try to boomerang us out of here. Why don't you blast that music."

I put Darlene all the way up. The Mustang drifted round the corner, then plunged into the valley. We shot down like a pinball, our eyes wild and frightened. We were shouting to the track "All Things Are Possible!" I gripped the passenger handle, shouting with Mom as we plummeted, "All Things Are Possible!"

The Mustang flew right past the frail drawbridge over Wolverine Creek, then up we went, up the steep hill, more of a mountain within a mountain. Mom beat her hands on the steering wheel, chanting "Help Us Jesus Help Us." I leaned all the way forward like a long-jump skier. To our amazement, the Mustang rocketed up at full speed. We were laughing with surprise and hope, a kernel of relief.

Then three-fourths of the way up, Rocky lost traction. The engine kept failing to roar as we slipped down the mountain. Mom slammed the gas down, but the tires kept sliding down. I sucked in all the air I could to make me lighter. The Mustang kept fishtailing, Mom struggling to keep control, the car a couple feet from the ragged cliff with no guardrails. We kept falling down the mountain. For the first time that trip, I felt absolute terror. If we sunk to the bottom of Wolverine Creek, the snow would bury us before we could walk to the nearest house.

The chorus hit. Darlene going wild with her tambourine: "All Things Are Possible!/ All Things Are Possible!"

Mom adjusted her prayer. "C'mon Jesus, C'mon Jesus." I joined her. "C'mon Jesus C'mon Jesus" we shouted in unison.

A little past halfway down, the Mustang caught a dry patch. Or the engine finally kicked into overtime. Or, as it felt in the moment and as Mom would tell her friends for years to come, a miracle happened. It felt like God had placed his hands on the bumper of the Mustang, and pushed.

I do recall suddenly feeling like the Mustang was being pulled forward; or simply lifted, like we had clasped the lifesaver thrown overboard, and someone was pulling us in. Years later, Mom would say it felt like someone else was at the wheel.

We reached Grandma's house. My memory by this time blurs. We were so relieved to be past that final valley, amazed that a mysterious force had picked our tired Mustang up and helped us through the final hurdle. We were too stunned to do anything but tiredly laugh. "You're the best co-pilot," she repeated. We parked. Mom said we'd unpack tomorrow.

I followed Mom up the snow-smacked steps to Grandma's house. She was fiddling with some keys, then turned back to catch my eyes.

"See," she leaned toward me, her smile weathered and exuberant. "All things are possible."

It surprises me that all memory of that day ends here. I don't even recall seeing Victoria. The one-hour trip had taken five. The next day, we learned that 29 inches of snow had fallen in 24 hours, beating the 1955 record for the most snowfall in a single day by at least nine inches. We had sat at the edge of our seats the entire journey, terrified but excited, happy to be together, and harrowingly aware of death.

CHAPTER 2

House of God

Until Mom won custody, I traveled between Alaska and California a few times each year. This was between 2000 and 2003, when I was 10 and 13. I racked up thousands of frequent-flyer miles and enjoyed my special status as an unaccompanied minor. Flight attendants came to know me. They'd give me extra pretzels or sneak me into first class on red-eye flights. I made friends with other unaccompanied minors who traveled the same Pacific coast circuit, including Austin, a mischievous redhead whose practical jokes on adult passengers forced a flight attendant to separate us.

Post-divorce, Dad keenly expressed his own emotional crisis by buying a black Mustang. It was opposite to Mom's Mustang in several ways. The exterior was slick black, a '96 model compared to Mom's blue, nicked-up rendition from the early 80s. Its V6 engine roared, thrusting us along the I-95 like Apollo 11 astronauts. The Alaska Mustang moved along fine, but its V4 was nearly inaudible and triggered envy from no one.

Dad's seats were fine black leather that smelled polished and new. Mom's seats had feathery, matted blue seat covers; Lee Ann, my half-sister, joked that the Cookie Monster had been skinned alive for them. I unpeeled those seat covers just twice; they were sad, mud brown, with Miró-shaped stains of questionable origins. The seats smelled of damp hay.

In downtown LA, halted by traffic, Dad loved to rival the sound system of anyone else playing music loudly. We once sat next to a car blasting rap, a genre this LA Sheriff associated with foul play, and my father was determined to drown out the noise with his own sound system. He blasted what we happened to be listening to — "Get the

Party Started" by P!nk. The subwoofers demolished the noise of everyone surrounding us — putting them in their place, which likely remains my father's favorite pastime.

Mom's Mustang, in contrast, was everyone's. She let me choose the music. We picked up anyone who requested a ride. Mom listened to Lee Ann's hour-long monologues about boys on road trips to Fairbanks. I sat silent and petrified in Dad's car as he cursed the traffic in Burbank and blared Rush Limbaugh. We were always visitors in Dad's Mustang, but in Mom's Mustang we belonged.

When I was about one year old, a semi-truck moved into my parent's lane on a highway in California. Dad swerved, tumbling the car over a safety railing. We flipped a dozen times. When the car stopped, we were all upside down. Mom came to first. The car's leaking battery was inches from her face. She jerked her head to see my father unconscious. She looked back at me, hanging upside down from a car seat; there was a cut on my lip, but I looked unharmed. "You didn't cry then or later," she told me as an adult. "You just kept looking around, like you were surprised at what was going on. Your eyes were real big."

We were taken to a hospital. Someone fetched Lee Ann from kindergarten. Dad suffered damage to a several spinal discs; the pain never totally subsided. Other than some bruising, Mom was unscathed. Considering the total wreckage of the car (I never asked my parents the make), we were amazed the damage wasn't worse. By any physical measurement, we were lucky.

For Mom, it was a religious re-awakening. I'm now her age then — 29. I can imagine the extreme need to react to such a close call: had that battery touched her, her face would now be disfigured; I could have died from a glass shard angled to my throat; her husband could have been confined to a wheelchair for the rest of his life. Our luck, to Abby, could only be explained by God.

My father hadn't married a very religious woman. At 21, he had married a woman who liked short skirts and lipstick and motorcycles. Yes, she had been raised Pentecostal where women wore ankle-length dresses and their hair past their waist, but she'd become more secularized in her mid-teens, watching MTV and rollerblading to Donna Summer. But after that accident, everything changed. She returned to the roots that grew long before my father came along. They had kept their lives after the accident, but their marriage had entered the beginning of a long end.

Mom took us to a nearby Pentecostal church until Grandma objected over doctrine. I think it was about the order of operations when it came to salvation. Victoria believed one could only get *truly* saved by following Acts 2:38 to a T. This meant one had to repent, then get baptized, then receive the gift of the Holy Ghost. The first church Mom took us to believed that someone could start speaking in tongues before they repented, if that's how their relationship with God unfolded. But Grandma maintained that this wasn't what the Bible said. Compounding this effrontery was their diction: this church used *spirit*, in accordance with some updated translation of the Bible. If they *truly* wanted to be saved, they had to use the word *ghost*, as it was written in the King James Bible. Mom listened to her mother, and switched churches to one that unerringly followed Acts

2:38: *Then Peter said unto them, Repent, and be baptized every one of you in the name of Jesus Christ for the remission of sins, and ye shall receive the gift of the Holy Ghost.*

Fortunately, when it came to Pentecostal churches, Mom had the pick of the litter. In some respects, LA County was the birthplace of modern Pentecostalism, with fiery bombshells like Aimee Semple McPherson getting her start around the arid valley in the early 1920s. As Joan Didion observed in *The White Album*, "In the interior wilderness no one is bloodied by history, and it is no coincidence that the Pentecostal churches have their strongest hold in places where Western civilization has its most superficial hold. There are more than twice as many Pentecostal as Episcopal churches in Los Angeles."

Abby settled on a small church in Sylmar, California, a 20- to 30-minute drive from our home in Canyon Country. The congregation of a few dozen people met each Sunday and Wednesday in a house-turned-church in the midst of a residential maze. The church had a DIY spirit where the performance of substance was more important than substance. Its philosophy was at once strict and malleable: deeds mattered less than what was in the heart.

I was baptized at eight in a horse trough — not that the setting mattered because what counted was the unknowable, solo connection one had to God, which, mysteriously, could only be proven at a public altar.

We ended up falling in love with the megachurch in Santa Ana. The drive was over an hour, so we'd only venture so far south if we were looking for an experience not unlike that found in amusement parks. The facade, when I was about four feet, seemed several stories high. Glass walls shot up like geysers, frozen like some spiritual aperitif. There were hundreds of pews – feast table long – as opposed to the protean pews of Sylmar. Sylmar could fit 45 people max. Santa Ana could seat 1,000 at any single moment. Seats opened up as segments of the congregation stood to jump up, dance, or faint in the aisles.

I recall none of the sermons at Santa Ana. I recall a white man in a white button-down suddenly shooting up and sputtering "HAllelUjAH!" Several others, all men, likewise inspired, rocketed upward. Instantly, the mammoth choir stood; the orchestra played *sans* conductor. The entire congregation rose, clapping and shouting and falling on pews; picking themselves up, clasping their hands in tears and abjection, fearful and crazed in the grip of imagined hellfire. The first young man who had yelled "Hallelujah!" ran laps around the church's perimeter, his arms raised high like Caitlyn Jenner on the Wheaties box. Others followed suit, creating a running platoon that now reminds me of M★A★S★H.

I'd mimic these men. There was a prayer room somewhere in the complex. With lengthy interrogation-style windows, men (why was it always men?) paced the space, visibly praying hard. They clapped their hands in private conniptions, suddenly jutting the air with the back of their hand, as if slapping away Satan. I'd follow the literal steps of these men. Like them, twisted in private argument with God – caught in their own drama of Jacob wrestling with the angel – I'd shake my tiny fists and shoulders and swat the air just like them. It's this image of my small form following these men in earnest prayer that stayed with Mom. She must have known it was performance on my part, but a larger part of her was thrilled that I was learning. One day, these gestures wouldn't be pretend, but severe and authentic commitments to my belief in God. She smiled, assured in this image, this suggestion that one day my praying would be real.

I liked to dress up for church, whether Sylmar or Santa Ana. Victoria, when she visited from Alaska, delighted at my display. "Little Pastor Matthew!" she'd squeal. Hearing that I was the only little guy in Sunday School to really remember Bible verses, the pastors began to groom me. "Pastors do this, Pastors never do that" — small comments that were meant to determine my life. But their mentorship was somewhat pushed by Abby. I don't believe their heart was ever in it, perhaps sensing my essential perversion, or simply fearful of their job security. The pastors never called me "Little Pastor Matthew," as Grandma did, but gave me the standardized salutation that all of God's children were entitled to: "Brother Matthew, good morning!"

Brother Matthew was a sobriquet that followed me through Wednesday night Bible study, Bible camps, and equally raucous services around Sylmar, Palmer, and Anchorage, all the way up to when I left the church at 15. By then, it became evident, even for Victoria, that a pastorship wasn't in my future. She started to call me *mijo* more, or simply Mateo. From her fellow congregants, Mom heard less and less of "And how is Brother Matthew?"

At 13, I said *I'm gay* aloud to myself in the shower. I was trying it out for fit, having suspicions this was the case since I was eight, and certain memories from four and five. The words had meaning, and I found myself repeating in horror *I'm gay* more than thirty times. The world closed in on me, and I sat down under the running water. I cried unconsolably. Realizing I was gay was like suddenly knowing a life-threatening disease had been burrowing itself through my bones for years. I was terrified at how quickly it would make me rot, and profoundly disgusted with myself for not knowing that all this time I was diseased.

Quietly, I willed myself straight. I dated a couple of girls. I looked at straight porn and told myself I was imagining being the guy. It wasn't so much that I wanted the man's biceps and asses and spritely schlongs; it was that I simply wanted to be like them.

But as I started to question the church's paradoxical stance on so many things, I began to wonder if being gay was such a bad thing. At 14, I googled for a chart listing the differences between Republicans and Democrats. I was shocked to see that everything I was in favor of was not favored by the party I grew up believing in: funds for the UN, the right to an abortion, gay marriage, assault-weapon bans, protection for the environment — these were causes taken up by the political family I was taught to rank slightly above Hitler: the Clintons. But after that chart, my fundamental beliefs loosed as baby teeth, every news article wiggling the ragged tooth from its conservative mooring.

I continued going to church and passing out pamphlets, saying I loved Christ even though I probably was bi and he'd have to forgive me for that. I came across more material that made me question whether the real malice was within the church, rather than with *the gays*, as the congregation called them with rabid disgust.

The first confident gay kid I came across was in literature: *The Perks of Being a Wallflower*, which I read as I approached 15. Patrick gave me a model of what someone in my condition could be. That same year, *Brokeback Mountain* became a well-known film. Even when the library acquired a DVD copy, I knew I would never have the gall to check it out. So I settled for the novella by Annie Proulx, a pocket-size edition about 70 pages, which I safely read in a dusty corner in Anchorage's largest library, the Loussac. Those first few pages gave me the ripest erection of my life; I crossed my legs to obscure the evidence. An hour later, I was in tears. I had never known that love could exist between men, or that anyone could perceive my pain.

As I continued going to church, I wondered if this major component of who I was could be submerged for the rest of my life. Increasingly, I wondered about true kindness. Knowing that I likely was gay, I became attuned to the simmering hatred I hadn't noticed before: the assistant pastor who spoke each Wednesday of "The Virtuous Husband" then pointedly looked at me when saying a holy relationship could only exist between a man and a *woman*; the glint-eye pastor who unfurled a wall-length map of hell to detail what happened to homosexuals in the sodomite quarter of hell; another grizzled beard pastor who said it'd be better for gays to kill themselves rather than spread the contagion of their faggotry. Suddenly one Sunday, I simply told Mom that I would not go.

Maybe once a month I would go, but I felt on edge the entire time. One Sunday I caused a stir by adamantly refusing to leave the car. I felt guilty that Abby had to go to church alone, but I could not go to a church that harbored a tacit giddiness should all gay people suddenly die.

By 16, I stopped going altogether. Even for Easter or Mother's Day. The excitement of me dressing up for church became an isolated memory. There was no hope of revival. Mom and Victoria both were deeply disappointed, I imagine. Here and there, Mom would ask if I wanted to join her and Victoria. I said no, and she'd reply in her sweetest voice, "All right then, if you change your mind, give me a call."

They could have made me go to church. They could have been harder with their punishments. The glint-eyed pastor, I'm sure, reaffirmed that this was in their right.

But as with so many times when it came to the case of me, they relied more on prayer and love.

CHAPTER 3

Shotgun Wedding

Farm Loop is miles of flat farmland north of Palmer circled by a loop road; I never knew which came first: the farm, the loop, or the name. All I knew for certain was that on Sundays we were to drive from Lazy Mountain to join a Pentecostal church in Farm Loop, no questions asked.

I learned in middle school of the Dena'ina who lived along the rivers of what is now called Anchorage, but nothing about whoever was first to live in Palmer and Wasilla, the region now called the MatSu Valley, *Matanuska* being a bastardization of the Russian *Matanooski*, meaning "Copper River People." I learn now that the Copper River People are Athabaskan, a language group I've heard of, specifically of the Ahtna tribe, which I've never heard of. The Ahtna primarily lived along the Copper River, some 200 miles southeast from the valley settlers named after them. Such is the accuracy of colonialization.

Under The New Deal, 1,000 or so settlers traveled up from Minnesota and Wisconsin and Michigan to farm the unappetizing land. But the area turned out to be fertile, and under the midnight sun, vegetables grew four times their expected size. This is a theme with Alaska: what first appears inhospitable can become nourishing; middling expectations will be outshined by the unbelievable reality. The settlers were by and large pleased and chose to stay. Some of these folks eventually converted a farmhouse to a megachurch and called it Farm Loop. It was to be non-denominational, but the people who kept showing every week were 500 Pentecostals.

I remember Farm Loop most vividly for the New Year's Eve services, where hundreds of people prepared for the end of the world. I also remember the vague, repetitive sermons delivered in five-minute spurts. These lecturers seemed mandatory, even as everyone understood that the best way to express our love of Jesus was song and dance. Each Sunday was like a music festival: groups of fiddlers were featured, then female acapella singers, then some dude with a grisly voice, an electric guitar, and acute knowledge of five chords. For regulars, just thinking of Sunday stirred their spiritual tumescence.

Abby met Caleb at Farm Loop. He was a full-cheeked fellow with blonde, cherubic hair. He had a stern body at 5'8, two inches shorter than Mom, and he liked to show off the biceps he built from 200 daily pushups. He was 21 when he started being extra nice to Mom. Stray acquaintances and the youth groups, which Caleb occasionally joined, whispered that this was his way of getting to my half-sister: butter the mother up. Grandma was the first to divine his true intentions, her own history of dating younger men perhaps guiding her forecast. No one at Farm Loop thought it odd that Caleb would be interested in a 16-year-old girl, but they needed a minute to imagine a 41-year-old female with a man two decades younger.

I must have met Caleb in the winter of 2001, then again in 2002, around the St. Patrick's Day Storm. Dad had already remarried, just a couple of months after the official divorce in April 2001. At the time, I thought Mom was simply responding to Dad's quick rebound. But it was never in her nature to get even. For her, vengeance truly was the purview of God. She only saw Caleb as a friend, and that's how she presented him. Had I viewed him as a prospective stepfather, my judgment would have pointed out the obvious signs that made him a dud: he rarely showered after the gym; he stooped around the world like an awkward high schooler; he could only find work as a cart-pusher. As an 11-year-old, even I knew this man was dim-witted.

I learned that Caleb fancied Abby through a postcard. Mom sent the perfunctory note in April 2002, exactly one year after the divorce. That my family had spiraled into non-materiality in less than a year intensified my reaction to Mom's new relationship. I suppose the best word for my reaction is *horror*. How could she move on from us so quickly, I demanded. Years later, once I understood my father's character, I was amazed she didn't flee sooner. But during the divorce, I didn't understand why she left us. On the phone, I begged her to come back. I demanded it, cried for it, yelled for it. I tried to manipulate, saying that I broke my nose playing basketball and I needed her back in California to help me get better. I felt that my mother did not love me enough to come back. Faintly, I knew that my family was broken, and I fell asleep crying. I overheard my father once talking to Abby on the phone, trying to do her some harm: "You have a little boy who cries himself to sleep every night. What the hell are you doing up there?"

I called her with that postcard shaking in my hand. "How could you be dating *Caleb*?" I asked, exasperated. "He's weird and he always smells bad."

(The age difference hadn't entered my objection; I had always believed age was nothing but a number, and my belief was supported, perhaps, by Grandma's relationship at 71 with a man of 33).

Mom demurred: "Oh you know, we just like spending time together. We're seeing where this will go."

I was mad at her for moving on so quickly and told her so.

"Well. I am sorry you feel that way."

I'd get to know Caleb that summer of 2002, often in drives to Farm Loop. It's how the two of them bonded, too. I forget why, but Caleb picked up Abby from Lazy Mountain and drove her to church. Or he broke a leg and couldn't drive (that's it), so she became his chaperone. And Mom, having a life-long affinity for any big machine from motor country, was overjoyed to drive his hulking Ford. That she was traveling with a handsome man who wanted to go to church must have been a rare reprieve for her. She was most comfortable being needed. Caleb, as invalid, gave her something to care for.

Caleb was a sensitive, God-fearing man. He likely opened up to Abby easily. She had that effect on people, especially troubled souls who rarely encountered the caress of absolute attention. "Attention," Simone Weil has observed, "is the highest form of prayer." Abby gave meaning to that old cliché: *to lay eyes on someone.* When she looked at you, it was with the gaze of pure prayer.

Caleb's dad was a misanthrope who lived alone in the dense woods out of Wasilla, Alaska. He had hit Caleb with belts, cutting boards – once with a frying pan on the head. Caleb's mother, Danielle, was Abby's age – just as good looking as Mom with the same slower, considered movements and social graces, but with none of the compassion. If Mom belonged in *Little Women,* Danielle belonged in *The Fountainhead.*

But Mom needed to be needed; Caleb needed someone to listen and provide the singular care and focus that his own parents had refused. They were perfect for one another. In one of my cheerier moods, seeing how Caleb regarded my mother, how she perked up around him and gained the light-weight happiness that was absent in California, he didn't seem so bad. I even said (feeling it false at the moment but wanting to please her):

"Mom, I think Caleb 's just what the doctor ordered."

She turned to me with bright eyes. "Really?!" She looked like a kid whose parents had suddenly changed their mind on ice cream for dinner.

I nodded my head, then a 13-year-old, with great sagacity.

"Yes. I really do believe that."

I never believed that. I came to know Caleb as an absolute fool. In one journal entry, I cogently call him "an idiotic idiot." They weren't good for each other, Mom and Caleb, but even under my intense hatred of a stepfather one decade older than me, I understood that they needed each other.

At first, my dislike of Caleb was all superficial. The boy smelled. After 90 minutes of running laps around the pews, whooping and hollering and shaking his hands with the Mighty Knowledge of Jesus, he was bound to produce some serious BO. In the lobby, I'd watch him place his stout leather jacket over his wife-beater. He wore black fedoras and brown cowboy boots. His leather jacket had fringes along the underarms. I flinched each time I saw him.

Over the summer, I'd learn just what low voltage charged Caleb's brain. He'd talk about drilling ANWR. It was all a conspiracy, he told me; no animals would actually be harmed, as many of them didn't even live above the Arctic Circle. He wanted the state legislature to release the entire wealth of the Permanent Fund Dividend to all Alaskans at once, so instead of the annual $1,000 check, every man, woman, and child would receive a few million dollars. It would leave nothing for future generations, but Caleb thought they should be able to fend for themselves and that people had to right to live in the moment. When he learned that I used to be really into dinosaurs, he informed me that the evidence of their existence was flimsy at best. I won't ridicule the guy by strolling out each stupidity I happen to recall, but I will say that Caleb liked to cut his toenails two inches from his face. Once hunched over, clipping away like a mad scientist, a big chunk of toenail flew straight into his eye. He yelled. Mom fetched the tweezers.

That summer, Mom tried everything to get me to like Caleb: movies, skateboarding, chess, video games, candy. But I got no closer than my first impression of him as a sweaty pseudo-cowboy who couldn't fire a pistol. I hated the prospect of their relationship, which probably explains Mom's hesitation in telling me that they were going to marry.

We were in the Mustang, driving up and down through slimming streets covered by canopies of twisted oak, the world a deep green from the summer's constant sun.

"That's great!" was my first reaction to the fact that my mother was getting married. Then I remembered it was to Caleb. I swiveled to her from the passenger seat. "Please don't do this. Please don't marry Caleb."

For the next couple of minutes, I outlined why a union with Caleb was a poor idea: they'd known each other for less than a year; he was immature; he only ever held down part-time jobs; he had twice as much credit card debt as she did; hardly any time had passed since moving on from Dad.

"It's too late," she said, with tiredness I rarely saw in her, a mixture of uncertainty and conviction, and perhaps sorrow that this was how I truly felt. "We're due in Anchorage in about four hours."

We turned into an empty dirt lot. The strip mall had a bridal store. Its windows were expansive, but the tense sunlight only accentuated its layers of dust and gunk and mud. Lee Ann was already there, perhaps driven there earlier by Caleb. She could easily forgive those who weren't good to Abby, and was on good terms with Caleb. Lee Ann spun around in a mauve maid of honor dress with a gigantic smile. And me, I was to be Caleb's best man.

Half an hour later, I was wearing a white tuxedo and riding with everyone else to Anchorage. The tux was over $400, probably two weeks' worth of Mom's take-home salary as a dishwasher at Vagabond Blues Cafe. I knew it was stupid to buy such an expensive tux for a shot-gun wedding; $400 – serious money to us – for a garment that I'd wear in public only once. But I was 12, and it wasn't my wedding day.

The drive to Bethel Chapel isn't with me now. I was numb all the way to church. Not until we were standing at the altar before a charlatan pastor does my memory kick in. He was proclaiming that God, in his great and unmatched wisdom, had clearly meant for these two to be together. This was the right direction for them both, he said. The 15 people who could make the same-day wedding nodded. Then the pastor thundered: "From this day forward, you will no longer be known as Abigail Ruth Caprioli, but as Abigail Ruth Olson."

I bit my cheek. The congregation seeing me likely attributed the stone tears and inert face to the unsuspected happiness attained through a righteous union that a child could not possibly understand — but feel. This union was holy, unlike the one my mother made in her first youth, with my father who, as a Catholic, was inherently damned. In actuality, I was crying because I would no longer carry the same name as my mother.

The reception took place at a Golden Corral. The honeymoon was at the now defunct Fifth Avenue Hotel. I thought it was a magical opportunity. We rarely stayed in a hotel so tall — four flights was unprecedented! More often, if lucky, we stayed in a Motel 6 with two stories max and a clean-ish pool. But the 5th Avenue Hotel — now that was elegance: dark green and slick black color schemes, HBO, room service. Caleb and Abby informed the front desk that they were just married, and we all were given rooms on the "penthouse" overlooking the runways of Merrill Field Regional Airport. I didn't know that the rotating sign of a caricatured woman, something like Jessica from "Who Framed Roger Rabbit," was a strip club. I also didn't know that the squat, corrugated building behind the hotel was also a strip club called The Show Boat. Or that Fantasies, a block away, was not a video arcade. At 18, my best friend and I chose to celebrate by legally buying porn for the first time. We parked at the Castle Mega Porn Store. I stepped out of the car and looked back to see the signage for the Fifth Avenue Hotel.

Mom rushed the wedding because she wanted both of her children present. I visited multiple times a year, but Lee Ann chose to come for some of the summer or Christmas, but never both. For Abby, it was marry Caleb now or wait another year for both of her kids to be present. Throughout our visit that summer in 2002, she must have gone back and forth on whether to marry Caleb. The day before we were to fly back to California, she pulled the trigger. I wonder if she ever regretted that spontaneity.

None of it was planned, like most of her decisions, but everything worked out. There was only time and money for rings from Walmart, which worked out well because Caleb knew someone with an employee discount. The Fifth Avenue Hotel was closer to the Ted Stevens International Airport than any place in the valley, so spending the night made logistical sense. Simple coincidences like this always pleased Abby. It gave her something to magnify so that the central discontentment around any incident appeared minor.

Lee Ann didn't want me to sleep with her in the queen bed, and truth be told, I'd rather sleep on the floor than in bed with my older sister. Which is what I did. Until 2:30am, when I thought the dresser could be more comfortable: it had leather padding and an accordion filing system that could double as a pillow. I didn't sleep well on the dresser. The room was huge, yet for some reason, there was no furniture beyond the queen bed. But I suppose the only point of a room at the Fifth Avenue Hotel was the bed.

By 6 a.m., I had given up on sleep. I stepped out to the frigid morning. The sun glinted on the frosted runways of Merrill Field. Mountains to the north brandished their pointed tips in audible waves. The grays were choosing which colors to become, each their own rhythm and chime.

I walked along the empty hotel patios. All of the curtains were shut. Pig-sized ravens croaked in the streets. The fleet of cars in the Toyota dealership was intricately frosted, but the corner windshields had been scraped to keep the prices red and loud. A slew of contrasts gripped me: the celestial sky compared to where Caleb and Mom had exchanged vows 15 hours ago in the seemingly holy church, some seven blocks from these strip clubs and porn stores; that Mom's rebound marriage was not totally void of happiness; that a city alive with nearly 300,000 people could be near dead in the early morning, that the mountains defining Anchorage were emblems of safety and danger.

I felt terribly desolate that morning. Mom and I no longer shared a common name. She was rooting herself elsewhere, gone in some vital way that no one could restore. Wandering around the hotel alone, it all suddenly felt that freedom had become obligatory.

CHAPTER 4

Desert Rose

In early August 2019, I landed in Southern California to celebrate a childhood friend's birthday. I had known Julie since 7th grade, when we sang "Let the Sunshine In" during recess and trash talked our mutual bullies. Throughout my visit, Julie and her boyfriend, Art, offered to act as chauffeur. Their kindness surprised me; the Californians I grew up with were so libertarian that I am still mildly surprised when people hold the door open. But Julie and Art were raised in Valencia and Val Verde, towns generally richer and literally greener than Canyon Country.

True to name, my childhood neighborhood sprawled up, down and around a canyon. It was all one-story houses. Canyon Country maintained a distant feel. Not a country feel, as there were too many people nearby and too little wildlife. But distant. Suburban. Too cowardly to be intimate and too needy to suffer isolation.

We drove up Soledad to visit 29701 Mums Drive, the house I lived in from 4 to 11. The route was impressively ugly. Scorched earth everywhere. Art repeated twice, trying to summon good cheer, that he had never had a reason to visit Canyon Country. Julie grew unusually quiet. She took in the dull surroundings. Signs for the public park were rusting, the grass beneath them mottled brown, a discoloration I don't recall growing up, probably because the dehydrated lawns of Canyon Country were home.

We passed miles and miles of houses, each imperceptibly different. Without a map, I directed Art through the steep hills to the cul-de-sac that was my first neighborhood. I wonder now if my good sense of direction comes from growing up in the middle of thousands of identical houses.

Since I couldn't rely on external cues to tell me what was what, my body became its own compass.

The cul-de-sac was just as I remembered, but smaller. More confining. I could not imagine how and why Mom had agreed to remain here for so long.

We drove slowly round the neighborhood. I pointed out the house marked by a giant willow tree; the owners couldn't sell it for a year, so the kids turned the empty pool in the back to a skate park. There was a squat, spinach-colored house recessed deep into a driveway, concealed from public view by a consortium of trees and weeds; that's where Chad lived, a boy a few years older than me with an angular jaw and blue eyes that fixed themselves in my dreams. The car, even driving slowly, was moving too fast. There's always more to tell beyond the allotted time.

So I stuck with the more discernible tales. I told them that the yellow ranch house with a scraggly chain-link fence once housed Cynthia Buckwick, who wanted to be a witch and, as an adult, hounded me about buying candles from her e-commerce shop and who, willing or not I'm unsure, was institutionalized. I told them of the trio of wiener dogs who lived in the plum-colored house who'd often escape and attempt to chase the postman. Then the house next to mine, the one I thought of as Danny's house, the only Mexican family in the two-dozen house cul-de-sac. Then Darren, a disgruntled white man of 35 who'd spray kids riding their bikes with a water hose then claim the damn kids were riding on his lawn. The 60-year-old, Rita, with her lava-dyed hair who sat on her porch most days with a sour-pinched mouth, hoping for yet scorning the prospect of company; Mom occasionally baked sugar cookies for her, which always triggered Rita's smile. The older man no one knew who died. His family quietly and quickly threw out most of his belongings, including mounds of *Playboys* into a recycling bin, which was promptly raided by me and Montana, my fellow eight-year-old and best friend whom my mother approved of for being a pastor's son.

That cul-de-sac was ripe for Hitchcock — quiet, uncanny uniformity. I saw clearly now that this was a place where people who did not like people set up. It was a place that believed in bloodlines, that the true north of humanity was evil and that the greatest hurt was being taken for a fool: it was far better to be bitter than trusting. It was a place for retreat after grave humiliation. Political bumper stickers were unnecessary. Here was the essence of conservative values: contraction of one's abilities, confinement of anyone else who questions too much.

We came face to face with this spirit on the edge of the cul-de-sac. I recognized him instantly. I never caught his name. To me, he was simply Jimmy and Johnny's dad, progenitor of the neighborhood's two great bullies. Johnny had punched me in the stomach so hard that I learned the phrase "knock the wind out of you" described the literal struggle for air. The younger one liked to whisper "fag" whenever we passed at the grocery store, in school hallways, on the bus.

Their father now eyed us from a shaded patio, giving Julie and Art – my good-humored friends in the arts and academia, the happiest couple I know – an audible chill. I smiled and looked away; his anger, I felt with relief, was no longer a part of my life. He, and by proxy his kids, could no longer harm me. But his glare has stayed with me, his instant alarm against all outsiders. That glare typifies the spite I grew up with, which was fed by my father and most of the blue-collar men on the street. He strikes me as a pathetic figure now, Jimmy and Johnny's dad with his lightless, wrathful eyes, clenched jaw, and bland crew cut. But growing up around that was menacing. I wouldn't wish spirits like that around my kids, and I can't imagine how Mom withstood it.

"I feel like," Art said with hesitation from the driver's seat, "we should get out of here." Julie nodded. I could have gotten out of the car. I could have told the man who I was, pleasantly asked if he remembered me, asked how he was doing. But even if he surprised me with a kind reception, I felt zero need to spend any time with him. My values want to give everyone a chance and follow Katharine Hepburn in *The Philadelphia Story* – "the time to make your mind up about people is never," – but I suppose that optimism gets smarter. Some people, you learn, aren't worth the effort; as painful as that can be, you have to move on. "Yes," I said to Julie and Art. "Let's." A part of me knew it was okay to be defeated. "Let's go."

I took a last look at the childhood home. It sat at the center of the cul-de-sac. It was the first thing you saw coming into the neighborhood and the last thing you saw if impelled to look back.

29701 Mums Drive was never a looker, with its wide garage door and window trimmings variations of muddled brown — sepia, umber, taupe. The exterior walls were of white, chalky stucco. This was a good and cheap way to absorb the desert sun, but the result was of a mottled paleness, not all that welcoming to look at.

But the current owners had fixed it up. I wondered how Mom would have mourned and celebrated the changes. A giant plant about 15 feet high had once stood at the base of our expansive lawn. I never caught the right name for this green desert tree. Everyone called it a bird of paradise, but I can't find online images of a bird of paradise that mammoth. Neighborhood kids liked to pluck off its thickly textured leaves. They'd fold one together along its crease to shape it like wings. Each leaf, about 4 to 9 inches long, became a sailboat. When everyone washed their cars on the weekend, we took these "boats" and raced them in the gutter, watching them sail fast away with the soap and spume of the current, feeling no guilt when they plunged past the bars guarding the drains and onto another world. The new residents of my childhood home had uprooted that tree.

They also removed the rose bush beneath our kitchen window. Like the tree, both removals were aesthetically pleasing. But the excision of the rose bush panged me. Mom had loved watching the rose bush as she washed dishes, humming to herself. Looking back, that rose bush was her resilience: desert roses stubbornly growing where they weren't meant to thrive.

The roses were never store-quality. The finest petals were thin and wilting. I don't recall a single rose from it that was a uniform, vivid red. The bush produced more thorns than petals, and I recall being stabbed by its thorns more than once while rescuing a soccer ball. But Mom kept watering the rose bush, and it kept churning out inexpert flowers. It only stopped growing once Mom left for Alaska and everyone was careless to its need for water.

My elementary school had the curious name of Sulphur Springs. That it wasn't named for a notable person or beautiful animal or anything more precious than the obvious amount of egg-smelling sulphur around speaks to the town's monotony. I can't blame Mom for rarely driving me to school, which was a 15-minute journey. Along with the inherent hell of school pick up, I bet many of the adults there weren't ones she fancied (or perhaps I'm projecting; she hung out with neighbors frequently enough, even as her body language with the majority of them suggested she'd rather be elsewhere). The drive back and forth was hardly scenic. You'd drive along the dried-up Santa Clara River, then several stand-alone gas stations, a couple of ranches I never saw animals on. It couldn't compare to the green fields and fresh lakes she had known in Michigan.

I mostly took the bus to school. I liked walking up the hill with my friends to the bus stop, talking about Pokémon cards and me pretending to like baseball. I liked how the bus driver, a woman in her 40s with Farrah Fawcett hair, clearly hated her job; we played a game of who could make her smile first — usually Arnold Schwarzenegger and Bill Clinton impressions did the trick.

I dimly recall Abby driving me on some rainy days, but I can only explicitly recall us driving to Sulphur Springs Elementary one time. I was 12 or 13. Mom was visiting from Alaska and had a rental car. Her father, whose entire career had been with General Motors, had nurtured her love of cars, and she knew how to handle a stick by the time she was 11. So I was at least a year behind in learning to drive and, without telling my father, she intended to change that.

Our drive to Sulphur Springs was practical, not sentimental. We simply needed a desert for drivers ed practice. My old school's backyard happened to fit the bill. I recall nothing about Mom's rental car other than it was an automatic. "You can learn stick in Alaska!" she excitedly informed me. (I'm stricken now that she rarely, if ever, said "I'll show you" or "I'll teach you." She offered, never commanded, which was kind, but showed an unfounded lack of confidence in her own skills to teach; this humility delayed some of the lessons I could have best learned from her).

My growth spurt was nearly complete. At 5'8," my foot reached the pedal. Mom repeated her caution to use one foot to command the gas and break. I told her it'd be easier using two feet. She nodded and said, "You'll see."

She was right about tapping the gas. The softest tap lurched the car forward.

"Whoa!" I said. Mom beamed with pride.

Once I could hold the car steady at 15mph, I floored it. The total power of our now speeding presence frightened and thrilled me; I laid off the gas as Mom cried *whoa there!*

I slammed the brakes. Our bodies flew forward then back like crash test dummies. Mom laughed. She looked at me from the passenger seat, no fear, looking more alive than I had ever seen her.

"You're just going to love driving."

When my father discovered Abby had let his 12-year-old son drive a rental car, he flew into a rage.

"I don't see what's the big deal!" She retorted. "There was no one around for miles. It's a weekend for God's sake. It's summer!"

Dad was eager to firm up each reason why I should live with him instead of her. *This* was why: she was an incompetent mother. "It's the principle of it, God damn it!" I can hear this fight clearly but couldn't tell you where it happened. "You're teaching him to break the law, Abby."

Maybe this was around 2003, during my sister's graduation. That would explain Mom's visit from Alaska, as well as Dad's increasing vitriol. He was loath to think of his new wife ever meeting his first wife. He forbade Abby from coming anywhere near the new house he bought in Castaic, a wealthier version of Canyon Country across the valley, but just as conservative. In one of these stressful schedulings, I recall eating at an IHOP with Dad and his father, who I loved, but never got close to. I forget what the conversation was about, but he spoke to her with utter scorn. The cellphone clenched in his fist looked about ready to break.

"Jesus Christ Abby, I already told you."

Mom wanted to see me or my sister. But according to my father, that was impossible.

"No. I already told you. What part of *no* do you not understand."

I heard her resisting on the phone. Dad ground his teeth. He clenched his other fist. At some point, he snapped his flip-phone shut.

"Fucking bitch."

Or was it "Stupid bitch?"

Either way, hearing my father call Mom a bitch was so baffling that I couldn't immediately feel the wound. But my grandfather knew. He looked at his son in disappointment.

"Don't say that about his mother."

Dad was too frustrated to reply. He kept glaring at the countertop. He excused himself to the restroom. We left soon after.

Try as he might, Dad couldn't keep Abby away from seeing her daughter graduate. But I don't believe Mom had anyone to celebrate with, except maybe a stepbrother who had driven up from San Diego, then turned around the same day. My father got his way: his new wife never encountered the first wife, and the rest of his family, who always preferred Abby, did not see her. How everyone would act in the life to come was all embedded at that high school graduation: my father's cruelty, my stepmom's rage, my sister's apathy, my relatives' helplessness to do anything, Mom's isolation, my near powerlessness.

My father's mother, Judy, had MS. She couldn't stand for long periods, so she and Grandpa brought along two lawn chairs. Dad's new wife barely hid her mockery; she spoke loudly, careless that anyone should hear her true thoughts: who brings lawn furniture to a graduation? Aren't they embarrassed? Is this not the epitome of white trash?

He listened to her rampages, nodding as if they were sensible, saying he'd see what he could do. She was a posh woman who had turned him on to designer clothes, gourmet food, sports cars. She was the worldly woman he should have married the first time around, and he found solace in her everyday cruelty. Mom, in contrast, would never think to criticize her disabled mother-in-law for hauling around lawn furniture. My grandparents sensed the new wife's judgment, and were uneasy around her.

Around my sister's graduation, I also discovered glimpses of her fundamental character. Though her mother had come down from Alaska to see her graduate, a trip of nearly 2,500 miles, I'm not sure they spent more than 30 minutes together — when Mom agreed to meet Lee Ann at In-N-Out Burger before Lee Ann had to hang out with her friends from Canyon High School. I sensed it was wrong, Lee Ann's indifference to Mom, who was so willing to do anything for her, but I tried to believe in Mom's own rationalizations: Lee Ann is busy; this is the last time she'll see many of her friends; she's young; she needs to have fun; there will be other visits.

Lee Ann subscribed to Dad's short-sighted and self-interested narrative that Mom was the one to abandon her children for Alaska. Lee Ann had been through her own fights and entanglements with Abby. While she learned much from Abby, she wanted to be her own person, in that fraught mother-daughter way I can only observe, if ever understand. She, perhaps more than me, felt reason to buy into Dad's dominant narrative. It may have been Lee Ann's total indifference, even occasional hatred of Mom, that redoubled my love for Abby.

I spent each moment I could with Mom. Along with driving for the first time in the desert near Sulphur Springs, we walked around Valencia Mall, Borders Bookstore, the new cinema in Canyon Country. When Abby lived in California, she took us frequently to this mall on the weekend, indulging in our pleas for pretzels with powdered sour cream & onion. Dad let me spend one night with Mom at the motel she found. He must not have looked closely at the address; had he, I can't imagine he'd accept the arrangement without a serious fight.

The motel was on the outskirts of Canyon Country. There were about 10 rooms in a nondescript gray building with an immense parking lot just off the highway. We checked in after sunset. Our neighbor, a scrappy blond man in his 30s, nodded to Mom's euphoric *Hello!* He sat on one of two mismatched lawn chairs, his feet on a blue upturned crate. A scratched-up boombox lay on the ground near a full cigarette tray. I don't recall if he was playing music.

We turned on the room's lights to find a Wild West themed room — silver belt buckles and stars, frameless photos of revolvers and standalone hotels like this one on dusty roads. The wallpaper alternated between strips of turquoise and fuchsia. The room was non-smoking, but the stench of smoke sat chained in the curtains. I peeled back some of the bedsheet to see a compact, juicy bug marching underneath. I shrieked and threw the cover back. Mom flung it back and killed the intruder swiftly with a tissue. Something moved in the corner. I turned to look under the desk and gripped Mom's shoulder. I pointed to a snake. Just a garter snake, poisonless and slender, but still a snake. Mom and I were terrified of snakes.

"Why don't we hop into bed," she decided. "Then have a nice, very early breakfast."

I didn't argue.

I slept over the comforters, convinced that there were more fat bugs underneath. I forget if Mom took her chances under the blankets. I remember we made up stories about royalty in an unnamed Eastern European country, silly stories about mistaken identities, or longings that seemed impossible until the very end. I forget exactly what we talked about. But what felt like hours passed pleasantly by with the person I liked most in the world. With her I felt safe, even as slim, poisonless snakes slithered beneath our beds.

CHAPTER 5

Figure Eights

First memory of Huntington Beach, California: around 2000. Mom takes me to a skating competition sponsored by Disney. This is the first time my competition isn't mostly 10-year-old girls. This is the first competition Dad watches.

I win the first round of Boys 12 and Under. I've never seen my dad take such interest in me; "Wow," he repeats, "I had no idea you could do all that."

But then we enter the Boys 14 and Under. These boys, mostly teenagers now, land doubles and even triples — spins I couldn't do even on my best days. I become so nervous that I fall seconds into my program, flat on my ass during a routine T-stop. I repeat steps in my program, forget essential jumps, and come in dead last out of this group of 20. I drift toward the skate's gate in uncontrollable sobs. I tell my family I need to use the bathroom. But I keep my blade protectors on and walk past the check-in and right out into the blistering sun. I sit on the Bravada's bumper and cry with my hands pressing my head like a trash compactor.

Dad finds me. He barks at me to look up. His gaze is unmitigated disgust. "Here," he says, tossing the dinky participation trophy my way. He announces we'll leave in five minutes.

Driving home to Santa Clarita, Mom asks if I want anything from Carl's Junior.

My father: "Really? You're really going to reward him for acting like a loser?"

She pulls in anyway. Dad and Lee Ann exit to eat inside. I don't want to leave the car, so Mom drives us through the pick-up window. She orders six-piece star-shaped chicken nuggets and apple juice; she knows my favorites without asking.

We park in the shade. I have rarely felt so much shame. I chew each nugget in soft bites, as if doing penitence with church wafers. Mom turns to me from the driver's seat. She pats my knee. "You know you're still my champ." Another wave of tears comes along, but I refuse to let the current pull me under. I continue staring down at my lap. A couple splintered inhalations, then inaudibly I mumble, "Thanks, Mom."

Second memory of Huntington Beach: 2002. We're driving from Santa Clarita to meet Dad's soon-to-be wife. He's finally come out to her with the fact that his son is not in college, as he told her the first few weeks they dated. His son is 12, and his daughter has to yet to graduate college, for she is 16. The impending wife, in her good graces, chooses not to dump him. She elects to meet the offspring. He is thankful for this.

We pull up to a large house along a man-made lake. The new woman is a lawyer; she only counts rich people as friends. Lee and I meet the other 12 people at the party. They find us endearing (we are trying to be endearing; Dad warned us to be on our best behavior). I love their polished skin, sharp watches, fine dresses and skirts, glimmering jewelry of weightful stone. We find the new woman to be admirable, cool even: put together, straight-backed, big-breasted.

It's potluck style. We all drift around, picking and nibbling at will, choosing who's worthy of discussion. Dad mingles with others, most of whom he doesn't introduce us to. Lee Ann and I stick together. At some point, the best friend of the soon-to-be-wife asks if Lee Ann and I want to use the kayaks. We spend the next 45 minutes circling the lake, laughing at various inanities, silently and completely impressed by the posh houses of this gated community, how — unlike Canyon Country — water and greenery are everywhere, and sports cars are the norm. Dad's new love interest: does she harbor a new, richer life for us? When Dad asks what we thought of the woman, we don't hesitate to say we love her.

Mom took me to an indoor rink in Wasilla several times during school breaks in 2001 and 2002. She would have taken me every day if my dedication to figure skating remained. But after the divorce, my interest in life collapsed. Outside of family troubles, the reason for my self-cancellation was rather simple: I was rapidly realizing that many of the things I loved — the Powerpuff Girls, Britney Spears, figure skating — indicated my sexuality. It was to avoid being called a fag that I stopped skating, the only activity I showed an uncommon talent for as soon as I hit the ice in early 1998. By 2003, I skated twice a month. I'd take pride in skating faster than anyone else with two hands in my baggy jean pockets. When no one was around, I'd practice jumps in the corner.

One early morning at the rink stands out. Mom had dropped me off before work; she'd pick me up during her lunch. The ice was nearly deserted, save for a mother watching her two girls, probably six and eight, skate around in stereotyped movements. They were adorable, but not particularly talented. I sensed this Other Mom watching me, admiring the power of my strokes, the quick grace of crossovers and three-turns in all directions. Under her appreciative gaze, I decided to perform.

I started my sit and scratch spins in the rink's center. I threw in a single-flip-double-toe-single-Salchow combo. I rolled through the reliably impressive footwork, culminat-

ing in a high split jump. Then (how it embarrasses me to say)
took one neon-green skate guard, and improvised a performance with my partner.

The partner was imaginary. On the other side of the
guard I imagined a girl holding my hand. As we moved into
a side-by-side figure 8, I held her close. In front of the Other
Mom, we danced a tango, which appeared to melt the Other
Mom into smiles. I threw my partner up for a jump, keeping
my eyes exalted as her body rotated three times. We zoomed
to the corner for side-by-side one-handed loops. When I
did a spiral spin, I held her hips as our bodies conjoined.
It saddens me to laughter at how desperately I wanted to
appear straight.

The Other Mom bought my performance. I was un-
tying my laces when she came over. She unrolled the usual compliments, and I replied with the standard modesty,
stressing that I still had a lot to learn. The Other Mom asked
why I was skating with a blade protector out there. I told
her about my skating partner down in California. I was a
pairs skater, I explained; yes, I enjoyed it because I got to
skate with my best friend. By how my eyes glistened at her
invented name – Caitlin – I hoped that Other Mom would
glean that I nursed a hopeless crush on this Caitlin. By how
Other Mom smiled, I believe she bought my performance.
And I was pleased to see her imagining prepubescent love;
I was pleased to see this Other Mom happy as she imagined
exactly how my life would unfold — pleasurably predictable
as a fairytale.

I was crazed by skating. I practiced footwork and loop jumps
for hours in the living room. Mom was willing to take me

to Pasadena, a 40-minute drive, for private lessons or hours of free skate three to five times a week. I started winning competitions, and a couple of coaches said at this rate I could go far. I idealized Michelle Kwan, Katarina Witt, Tara Lipinski; I wanted to be Michael Weiss, Timothy Goebel, Evgeni Plushenko. It's hard to remember that at one time I didn't think it was odd when I stretched my leg far above my head while skating backward to Bach or The Beach Boys in a flowing white chiffon pantsuit with a golden breastplate.

Looking back, I smile at the firecracker of a child who was astoundingly, blessedly gay. But by 12, I retreated from figure skating. I was realizing the ramifications of being gay in a history of people who considered fags worthy of burning. I closed myself off to everyone, especially myself. Like thousands of others, millions of others through history, I didn't follow through on what I wanted – what I was uniquely talented at – because of homophobia. I have sympathy for this 12-year-old who quit figure skating rather than be seen as gay. But that I didn't pursue what I loved, this activity that still makes me so alive, is one of my deepest regrets.

Mom took me figure skating for the first time shortly after I watched the 1998 Olympics in Nagano, Japan. With belly against the drab carpet, palms holding my head, I couldn't look away from the grace (and drama) between Michelle Kwan and Tara Lipinski. I loved the audacious backflip of Surya Bonaly, the divine spins of Chen Lu. I loved the passive-aggressive comments of Dick Button, the cartoon-ish outbursts of Scott Hamilton seeing Tara Lipinski land a triple-toe half-loop-triple-Salchow toward the end of her long program when most skaters are fighting exhaustion. The men's side interested me too, but it was the unrestrained passion of female figure skating that sparked my joy for the sport (the dudes restrained themselves so as to remain "the dudes").

We drove to the nearest rink, a run-down one in Burbank, some 30 minutes away from home. Mom got us our brown rental skates with dull edges. I laced them with the focus of the professionals I saw on TV. I stepped on the ice, nearly fell, but grabbed the wall in time. I replayed all the images of my pros charging out onto the ice. I took a deep breath, and mimicked them. Then just like that, I was skating.

Before my first lap was up, I wanted to try a jump. Something like the Axel. I raised my arms and jumped from my left front edge to the back edge of my right foot. I looked to Mom. Her jaw had dropped.

We stayed for another 20 minutes until my sister, who had been clinging to the wall, took a step unsupported and plummeted to her tailbone. Her pain was so severe that Mom took us to the ER. Lee Ann had some bruising on her ass, but nothing, fortunately, broken. I recall Mom talking to a nurse. The two of them agreed it sure was a good thing that Lee Ann had her hair up in a tight bun, as it would have cushioned the impact of crashing backward on her skull. This what-if scenario gave me pause. Lee Ann had not hit her head. Yet Mom and a nurse seemed more interested in the potential disasters avoided than in discussing the reality of falling on one's butt.

The short glimpse of what I could do on ice convinced Mom that I needed lessons. Thus began the constant battles with Dad over money: whether $450 figure skates were necessary, whether group lessons were subpar to private ones, did my skates need to be sharpened every other month, could we forgo buying costumes and just rent them, and why not only enter the big competitions where I'd be up against other boys. Mom conceded some standards, and peace was tentatively kept. But what made Dad crazy were the bounced checks. He'd rail against her careless spending. Mom mostly parried his frustrated pleas. She considered bounced checks to be a trivial inconvenience on her son's path to happiness. She'd point to other families who sacrificed for their children; some even took out a second mortgage. I forget how Dad responded to these extreme comparisons. I imagine none too kindly.

Dad didn't want me thinking this flamboyance was normal. Until I started winning competitions, he was rather disappointed by my figure skating. I was 10 when he first took me to a practice, Mom now living in Alaska. He'd hang out with the hockey dads as I practiced in the coned-off corner with all the female figure skaters. When I came up after practice, he'd start a conversation with the nearest hockey dad. "So this guy is starting to win competitions," he'd say loudly. "What are you working on now son? Some double toe-loop-triple-flip-who's-it-what's-it?"

I recall overhearing his worry in the kitchen, his angry fears that his wife was turning his only son into a "fairy." If I had to be small and fey, why not be a kicker, or even an outfielder? Masculine traits were important to him, and he wanted to transfer these "manly" qualities: men always keep their chin up, men can smell bad, men can scratch their balls in public, men were rascals. However unintentional, my father laid down my first conscious encounter with homophobia. I was four and, excited for being alive with my father, kissed him on the lips. He jolted back: "Matthew. Boys don't kiss boys on the lips."

Despite his demands, Mom kept me in figure skating. It brought her joy to see me skating freely along the ice. I had found something I loved and was good at. She would never take that away.

During my first few years in Alaska, Abby always took me to the indoor rink at the Dimond Center. In 2001, we'd leave Lazy Mountain by 3:30am to arrive at the Dimond Center by 5am, where Abby reported to work at the bakery. I'd be the first one on the ice as soon as they opened at 6am. I'd skate for an hour before I exhausted myself. I didn't have a coach, so I practiced moves from past programs. It strikes me now that I didn't skate with any specific goal in mind, but that I skated to exist. The cold tightened my mind's alacrity. Spinning around the rink in total control of the direction I took made me feel, if not powerful, then secure and right in the world.

The impulse to skate is not unlike the impulse to write. I write to know what I think, to transmute meaning in the process of telling, then even more powerfully, in the act of reading it back, seeing a vision manifested in actuality, the pulsating mass of potential energy finally given the proper torque to overcome its inertia and, in the minds of others, move. I prefer to write in longhand. How similar to figure eights and swivels are the streamers of text I scrawl between blue lines. The page, like the rink, is mostly white. The rink records a history of actions once alive. Its markings depend on brief impressions, momentary burnings into a once unblemished surface. When the movements are clean and clear and true, then the markings are a kind of brilliance because they bring the astonishments of the past permanently into the present. In skating, as in writing, I thread through the moments of my past and present self, then I pull and hope for coalescence.

∭

Some people, especially my father, may characterize my mother's actions around 2001 as irresponsible. That opinion isn't entirely incorrect. Instead of riding with her in a freezing Mustang with one headlight every morning at 3am, she could have left me with other friends, enrolled me in a free summer program through church, or, most practically, waited six more months until she had a more stable life, then bring me to Alaska. But she did her best. And as wild as my unsupervised time in the Dimond Center Mall was, I would not have been happier any place else.

Mom happened to be homeschooling my 11-year-old form when she was working at the mall 5am-2pm. I was supposed to complete worksheet packets from a Christian program in Maryland once the library opened at 9am, but more often, I claimed I did all the work then spent my allowance on a matinee ticket to "Spy Kids" or played "Dynasty Warriors 2" for four hours at GameStop. I learned how to stretch a dollar far. Mom gave me $3 to $5/day for food (her employee status gave her family free admission to the ice rink). I'd come to know Wendy's Dollar Menu by heart. I found the best lunch deals at Round Table Pizza, the cheapest sandwiches on Subway's Kids Menu. Wandering around the mall all day, I made friends with security guards, a librarian, a cashier at the bowling alley who let me bowl three games for free until the owner realized what was going on. I spent hours looking at fish and turtles and puppies until a gruff clerk asked, "Yo kid. It's 11:30. Why aren't you in school?"

My wanderings were untenable, and eventually, Mom sent me back to California. From afar, she worried about my diminished love for ice skating. The divorce had sapped my interest in more things that I had realized at the time, and the fear of being seen as gay was so overwhelming that even if we had lived together when I was nearing 13 and about to quit, I'm not sure she would have been able to talk me out of giving up. I recall telling her over the phone that I was serious: I just wanted to quit.

"Now why would you do that?" She asked me. "You love ice skating."

She said I might regret giving this up. I told her I was confident that wouldn't be the case. She didn't mention the thousands of dollars she and Dad had invested in me, or the hours she had spent driving, watching, hoping for me to succeed. Her greatest fear for me was to give up on what I loved.

We dangled the prospect of me quitting through several more talks. I was adamant. I didn't want to continue. It was stupid, I told her. I charged her with pressuring me to keep skating, a pressure that was to her benefit only. That last accusation gave her pause. Her own religious childhood had been unreasonably restricted. Pushing kids into something they hated was as dreadful to her as restraining them from something they loved.

"I just don't want you to regret this," she repeated.

I was 13 and had a weak grasp on the concept of regret. It amazes me that Mom had spotted the potential regret simply by loving me; had I been capable of adopting her vision, perhaps I would have maintained the courage to see and grasp what I truly loved. But in this given life, quitting figure skating is one of my life's deepest disappointments; one of those regrets a stone's throw away from not listening to Abby more intently, or doing everything in my power to save her.

CHAPTER 6

V for Vendetta

When anyone asks about my Grandmother, I tell them about the time she shaved her head and painted a large red V on top.

She was 77. I was 16.

The three of us lived at 4681 Blackberry in Anchorage, Alaska. The complex had three levels, each painted raspy gray with a ribbon of hunter green at the top, trawling along like a figureless frieze. A petite V-shaped hanger sheltered the outdoor steps. In theory only did it protect us from the slicing winds. Each step had a black gripping mat, sticky as a mouse trap, that kept us from falling.

Another L-shaped building complemented our own L-shaped version. From aerial view, it looked like two Lego pieces about to clink. The courtyard had no gardens or communal tables, but two great dumpsters. Everyone was inured to the smell. The younger kids incorporated the trash into their play: freeze-tag around or between dumpsters, using those steel walls as a backboard for soccer; in the summer, they'd sit in their shadow playing Go Fish. Only looking back can I whiff at the sourness of Blackberry apartments and see its abnormality.

Yet life inside that apartment was always warm. As I encounter more rich people in this life, that's one thing I see poor people having going for them: warmth.

Mom lived in the dumpster-facing bedroom with Caleb. I lived in the bedroom facing a thin forest, which I walked through every day to get to high school.

Grandma Victoria's mountain house was too cold most days of the year. Consequently, she tended to camp out in our living room. She stayed chipper as Mom left for work,

I for school. Caleb, the deadbeat, occasionally worked at Walmart pushing carts, but spent far more hours locked in his bedroom playing video games, back hunched like a curmudgeonous vampire.

Grandma spent her days underlining the Bible and taking errant calls from friends and family scattered about the US. I felt bad that she should spend all day by herself. To stave off any loneliness, I checked out library books and DVDs for her. She was no master of remote controls, so I loaded the DVD up before I left and made sure the power was on. All she had to do was press the two arrows for *Play*. If she wanted to watch it again, she simply hit play again once the credits were over. In this way, she might watch the same movie three or four times before I got back from school.

Victoria loved movies, would often tell me about Saturdays back when you could go for a nickel. For the next decade our lives ran together; she'd squeak in reminiscence when I was 13 and surprised her with a movie ticket to the Dimond Center:

"Mateo! Do you remember when you took me to see that movie with all the action in it?"

"I do Grandma."

"Oh boy. What was it called again?"

"S. W.A.T. It was about a S. W.A.T team fighting crime."

"Oh yeah. Talk about action. I was just" – she clasped her heart – "the whole time. And you bought me popcorn. Remember that?"

"I remember."

"A big tub of popcorn. Oh boy. That sure was fun to eat popcorn and see that movie with my grandson."

"It was, wasn't it?"

One week, I brought her *V for Vendetta* from the library. Taking inspiration from Guy Fawkes and the 5th of November, the movie was Natalie Portman trapped in a near-future dystopia where the government monitors and controls all aspects of civic life. Those who object are tortured. This includes Natalie Portman, who, in a freezing torture cell, is mercilessly beaten, but not before the camera catches her beautiful, tear-stained face as gloved hands shave off her gorgeous brown locks. If I remember correctly, Natalie Portman becomes a revolutionary.

The story resonated with Grandma on several levels. She, much like Natalie, had to make a radical change before she could come into her own. For Victoria, it was changing her first name. She was born Emma Castillo in Jerome, Arizona in 1929 to a family of self-inventors, or perhaps, re-creators. Mercedes and Martin, her mother and father, were listed as "Mexican" in the 1930s US Census, but by the 1940s were "White." (The powers that be didn't know where to put brown people, and given the choice between white and black, they pushed white, as this would increase their representation in the census). Emma's last name changed four times because of three husbands and one long-term boyfriend. She married at 14 and had a couple of children with a man who'd die in WW2. She remarried to a Mr. Marquez and moved around Los Angeles County. By 1947, she was 23 with five children and no husband. At some point, she legally changed her name to Rebecca. But Rebecca was Victoria by the time she met my grandfather, Joseph, a man whose birth certificate lists his parents as *negro*. Discharge papers from the Navy categorize him as *negroid*. Joseph returned from the Korean War not to his home state of Ohio, but to Michigan, where he knew no one and passed as white.

The exact order of operations matters little to me in recalling Grandma's story. As do the precise facts or details, such as whether her palms really were placed on burning coal after she and another little girl were caught putting their hands in each other's' panties, or whether her grandfather really was a "full-blooded Aztec man" who in the

Wild West of America, abducted her grandmother, "a full-bloodied Englishwoman." It's the rocking motion and comfort of the tale that matters. It's the reality of her cadence in my memory. When I read the first few pages of *Living to Tell the Tale* by Gabriel García Márquez, I recognized her in the tall tales of a grandmother blending fact and fiction, but always delivering magic.

There was no obvious forewarning to the impact *V for Vendetta* would have on Victoria. I came back from school that day tired and eager to be alone in my room to watch a show and study. "Hey Grandma!" I called, sliding the hallway closet open to hang up my jacket.

The hallway gave a straight shot to the living room, where Grandma sat enthroned among pillows. She had completely buzzed off the lush red hair that most women in their late 70s would envy. Her head was now bald with a bright red V painted on it.

"Hi *Mijo!*" she called back, chipper per usual.

I looked at her. My neutral face stayed neutral.

"I'll be in my room."

I turned down the hallway, and planned to stay in my room until Mom got home. Grandma, in my mind, was always doing weird shit. This was just a typical gesture for Victoria; I didn't need to ask why. In thinking of her, I don't mean to ridicule beyond a gentle prodding, as her oddities were reactions to severe teasing growing up. Her family were the only Catholic *spics* in a town of white protestants. Once, in San Diego, Mom took a wrong turn and took us into Mexico. Grandma panicked. "Take me back to the USA! Take me back to the USA!" When a border guard asked her all laconic if she was a US citizen, she spat: "Of course I'm a US citizen. I was born in the US of A, and I am returning. Now hurry up and let us back in."

Her embrace of peculiarity took a sort of courage. I see her gimlet eyes, her body by turns clothed in leopard leotards and a purple poncho with a bright red headband. Now, I think, by God: to be that stalwart in your beliefs, tastes and fancies, despite a million naysayers — that is courage. I didn't agree with her on many things, mostly politics, but something no man, woman, or child could ever fault Victoria on was a lack of conviction.

Still, she was sensitive to judgment and found it easier to live far from people on a mountain outside of Palmer (population: 7,037), or to join ranks with equally cast-off groups: the Samoan Pentecostals, the Jews for Jesus, and a swath of sweaty people with porous religious affinities or cranky Baptists living on disability.

I was freshly 15 when I searingly realized how others saw Grandma. My tennis partner, James Henderson, was waiting for me in the parking lot at 4681 Blackberry. He played Gameboy in the backseat of an overpriced SUV while his mother typed some message on her Blackberry. Mom and Grandma were also in the parking lot, heading to one of Victoria's weekly doctor appointments. Mom was helping her mother with the seatbelt. I tried to sneak unnoticed into James's SUV, but she spotted me.

"Be safe," she called out and waved.

"Yo te amo mucho!" Grandma squeaked from the passenger seat.

I sheepishly nodded at them. James opened the tinted backdoor, and I quickly slid onto the leather seat. His face was compacted with laughter. He squeezed back tears.

The door closed. We drove off.

James was on the precipice of crying from laughter. "What was she *wearing*!" He placed a hand on his belly mound, rolling in hilarity. For the first time, I had undeniable proof of how others viewed Victoria. She was ridiculous. What with discordant colors, quixotic fabrics, jangling bracelets of topaz, and ruby. She was cause for embarrassment. I didn't play along with any sustained mockery, but I

wanted to keep James as a friend, so I didn't defend Victoria.
I likely responded with "That's just my Grandma" or the less
generous "Oh yeah. She's nuts."

The reasons for not only shaving her head at 77, but
also painting a red V on it were these: the V stood for Victoria, but also for Victory; red was the color of love, as well
as the blood of the lamb − and the blood of Jesus − which
was passion, compassion, justice, and vengeance. The V
was a literal shout-out to Natalie Portman as revolutionary. It was also a sympathetic rallying cry against tyranny, as
choppily perceived by Americans; *V for Vendetta* was successfully marketed to an American audience ignorant of its own
excursions into tyranny. "Freedom!" one poster declaimed,
"Forever!" With that red V on her now scruffy head, Victoria intertwined personal history, religious allegiance,
aesthetic devotion, and political will. In telling this story to
friends, I usually wrap it up by noting the quadruple enten-
dre. Grandma may have been "nuts." She may also have been
a genius.

CHAPTER 7
Spenard

I've heard tales of children driving their drunk parent home. There's an inherent drama: a reversal of the natural order of things, the offspring made caretaker too soon, everyone caught in a bad fate. This reality happens often enough. "I was the child who had to raise the parent" is a banner ad in pop psychology. I cringe at that advert because it seems too congratulatory: it forwards a dishonest reinterpretation of a life together. The outsized reality of oneself as victim inevitably shrinks the life on the other side; it makes the understandable impulses guiding the protector dumb and their mishaps the result of negligence.

It's tempting and perhaps accurate to say that I parented Abby. But I choose to think of it as I taught her certain things, just as she did for me, by living certain principles — love, goodwill, generosity. We learned from each other. At times, I felt that she didn't teach me anything at all, no practical skills or advice that a parent should impart, but then I inventory what's good in my character: all of it comes from her.

I drove my drunk mother home only once. I was 17, driving to school or tennis practice in her white Jeep Cherokee. She was working on the Slope: 2-3 weeks above the Arctic Circle, then 10-14 days to relax in town. Or maybe she was doing a call center job. Either way, she had, with a supervisor, four margaritas by 4pm. She called me in a slurred voice, asking for a lift home. I was about to study or practice or go to work — I forget what, but I know I responded as an ambitious, disgruntled boy. I made it clear she was wasting my time.

I picked her up from the strip mall that houses Title Wave books. We had recently moved from the Southside of Anchorage to a small studio off of Spenard. Caleb had cheated on Abby with a German woman one floor beneath us. That was it for Abby, and the two were finally divorcing. He moved out with the woman. She, in turn, left her husband and five-year-old son. Mom's assorted jobs made more money than Caleb's part-time gig as a cart pusher at Walmart, so Abby lost a couple thousand in the divorce; she'd have gladly paid more to get rid of Caleb. I was thrilled to be away from the dipshit, but the sudden loss of his rent and the depletion of Mom's savings meant we would move everything out of the Blackberry apartment the day after Christmas.

I doubt I understood what stressors were on Mom: a man she loved had betrayed her; she'd have to move her kid in the middle of his senior year; her lack of a bachelor's degree meant a flurry of labor-intensive, meaningless jobs. It was hard for me to empathize with her as the giant hole Caleb dug seemed to be asked for by none other than she.

Mom had to ask me for $1,300 (cashier's check only) to pay for the studio in a run-down area of Spenard. When I reacted to her stumbling out of a Mexican restaurant thoroughly sauced, I responded more in touch with my frustration and indignation than sympathy for her divorce or her own thwarted hope.

Mom slurred her way to the passenger seat, a ditziness swashbuckling her face. Her quasi-manager looked on bemused, the lust apparent in the upward tilt of his mustache. I had seen photos of him where his jet hair flowed past his navel, but today, he piled his hair beneath a green stoner beanie. I didn't get out of the idling jeep to pretend to greet him. He gave his name loudly. I replied with a curt nod. Soon as the door closed, I sped us away.

Driving to the studio shithole we now called home, I mostly thought of the dead shock of suddenly parenting the parent. The same feeling as when we drove to First National Bank in this same strip mall to withdraw $1,300 for the shit studio. $1,300 out of the $1,600 I had saved for college by working in a concession stand that paid $7.50 an hour.

I chastised Mom as we waited for traffic to ease up for a right-turn on Spenard.

"I can't believe I just got out of school and I have to drive my drunk mother home."

"Oh relax." She blew her lips and clapped once. "I work hard. I'm allowed some fun."

I did something violent. Maybe banged on the dashboard. Or maybe I just raised my voice. I wonder if I was able to articulate what I was feeling: that her needing the money I saved for college enraged me, made me feel helpless, that I had depended on her and she had failed me, and no amount of apologizing would make me feel better. I needed actions from her now as I became an adult. Not words. The fantasy life that she had promised me growing up – that you could be absolutely anything you want if you only believed and worked hard – was appearing false, and I could not articulate, let alone admit to myself, that my reaction to the collapse of such beautiful ideals was anger, hurt, and panic.

Our studio apartment lay off Spenard Road, a historically dodgy part of Anchorage. During both World Wars, Spenard became a popular destination for soldiers wanting prostitutes. When we moved there at the start of 2008, it had a reputation for lust and drug use, but also cool new sushi and Thai restaurants, cheap bowling alleys, gourmet cupcake boutiques. The porn stores and strip clubs and bars like Chilkoot Charlie's with its "underwear room" remained, but they intermingled with fledgling art galleries and bookstores and movie theaters/restaurants like the Bear Tooth, which, I still believe, has the world's best pizza and root beer float. I'd grow to love Spenard for blending the high and low, the sexual vibrancy of its bars and the fecundity of its art studios. But at the time, we lived on a street called Cope: abandoned laundry baskets, derelict swing sets, inoperable trucks with broken windows. Each time I drove on it, I felt that God was sending gales of comfort and laughter: cope with your situation, it'll get better; your situation is shitty and here I am reminding you to put up and cope.

Around 2013, I'd stumble on the history of Spenard through a plaque in an ill-lit corner of The Anchorage Museum. I read about Joe Spenard, a charismatic entrepreneur fleeing an unhappy life in Eastern Canada. Joe and a group of friends dynamited a crooked path through the woods to a lake — now Lake Spenard — where Joe envisioned building a resort. He owned the city's sole taxi in 1915, and thus a quasi-monopoly on transport to the secluded paradise. The resort burned down in 1917, but both the road and the lake still carry his name. Spenard Road is unnecessarily sinuous because Joe was impatient and didn't have a mind for grids, unlike the engineers who laid out most of Anchorage. I like the story of Joe Spenard because it shows someone taking what's been done to them and making something greater. Even if the final form is chaotic, it's quintessentially their own.

My memory of life on Spenard begins with the apartment door. It was thin as poster board, painted a medical white, and knife marks obscured the peephole. Below the oculus were even more scratches, some gouges. We lived across from a young woman. Every night between 10pm and 1am, she'd stumble with a new man down the hallway whose scraggly carpet bore the skunk of vomit, piss, and vodka. A few minutes passed before we heard her pant variations of *yes yes yes*; moans of *oh my god*, and commands of *fuck me, pound me,* and/or *fill me up*. The first few nights, Mom and I looked at each other with wide open eyes, a hand over our mouths, and giggled. By the weekend, we turned up the TV and went to bed with earplugs.

The situation wasn't ideal, but we were happier together than apart. I could still read to my heart's content. By 2008, I was wild about books. I had a teacher, now a friend, tell me it was okay to love literature. She bought me a thrift store copy of *The Hours* and recommended I check out *Someday This Pain Will Be Useful to You* by Peter Cameron. The title came from an adage of Ovid's, one I needed to hear then, and that still justifies the study of literature. *Perfer et obdura dolor hic tibi proderit olim. Be patient and tough; someday this pain will be useful to you.*

Pictures of that studio show books in jagged piles along windowsills, on top of a broken radiator. In one, I'm reading aloud from a library copy of Sherman Alexie's *Flight*. I'm skinny in baggy sweatpants and a red hoodie, zipped to the top because that studio was never warm. With Mom's love, the teacher's direction, the quiet within the apartment itself (at least before 10pm), I learned what real literature was: truth, beauty, life.

Mom was gone half the time, working as a maid above the Arctic Circle. But she was there when I opened my first college acceptance letter. Of the four schools I applied to, three had put me on their waitlist. This choir of optimistic rejections was justifying my lack of self-esteem. I was beginning to believe that for me, I shouldn't expect anything more than their regular envelopes with the printed seal, the staid tone saying we like you, but we don't love you. That Clark University sent a majestic red binder to our crappy studio – replete with a welcome letter in a pretentious font and an embossed notice for a scholarship – seemed like a dream come true.

"My baby's going to college!" Abby shouted. She jumped up and down. I stood there with a dazed smile as she used my shoulder to propel her jumps higher. "My baby's going to college!!"

The scholarship was only $5,000 a year. Tuition was around $40,000 a year. I felt relieved that all that work in high school had resulted in some success, but I knew instantly that this wouldn't be enough for college. The tedium of proving oneself wasn't over yet. The goal had shifted from getting into college to paying for it, a challenge our infinite optimism had never considered. I reminded myself to not be so concerned: we were below the poverty line, and everything I read said private schools would offer need-based scholarships when warranted. But in that moment, I was happy to see Mom more joyful than she had ever been. Even if the cause for celebration would come crashing down before too long.

With Mom gone two weeks at a time, I often had the run of the apartment. I passed the time in mischievous or curious ways. I toured the complex: 10 units with no second floor. We lived next to a vacant studio. There was no door, and the hinges were asymmetrical and cracked. When we passed it, we politely looked away, as if bypassing a guy missing two front teeth whom we didn't want to make self-conscious. But one day, I strode inside. I wielded a wind-up flashlight meant for emergencies. I saw used needles in the corner, several mammoth spiders on the rafters, then what may have been a dead raccoon. I was out of there in two seconds.

I didn't miss Mom. We texted or called every day. And living with her in the same room for two weeks at a time made her bimonthly absence a relief, potentially for both of us. I was now 18 and insistent on independence, but also insecure, pompous, and needy. My mood swings were volcanic. Were I Abby, I'd see these trips to the North Slope as more of a work-vacation.

I kept busy with a couple of part-time jobs. One was at NewsCorps, which distributed magazines and newspapers to grocery chains like Carrs and Fred Meyer. I picked up pounds and pounds of zip-bound magazines and books from distribution plants, then stocked them in hundreds of checkout aisles. I never spoke with the men there at the production facilities, who perhaps found me too effete. I tried getting more work at the factory, but the interview was cut short after I answered no to the he-man supervisor's inquiry of Do you have a girlfriend.

My direct boss at NewsCorp, Regina, liked to look at my crotch and place her hand far too long on my shoulder. The pay was near minimum, and I was not reimbursed for gas. But I stayed because I could take home up to 30 magazines a week, and popular novels, so long as I ripped the front cover off. NewsCorp is how I learned about *The Economist, Psychology Today, Details, The Atlantic, Rolling Stone* — namely that there was a world larger than my own and more aligned with my hopes. It was within reach. All I had to do was read up, then act.

Part of that action was making enough money to escape Alaska. Reselling the magazines I picked up for free seemed like a logical move. So one day, after 5pm when all the factory men clocked-out promptly, I took a few copies of every single porn magazine NewsCorp carried. I felt zero guilty going over my weekly allotment. I only stopped collecting magazines once the weight of 50 porn magazines swaddled in my arms was too great. There was a rave that weekend, and I intended to sell them all in the parking lot for sticker price.

For years, if I ever wanted to regale someone with an Alaskan anecdote, I might tell them about the time I made $200 selling porn magazines from the back of my car at a rave. But that is an untruth. I did go to the rave. I did box up the mounds of explicit material and sell a few magazines before the doors opened. I planned to join my friends inside for a couple of hours, then bounce at 1am, selling all the porn mags to high kids in the parking lot. Instead, I did what any eager, horny 18-year-old would: forget all his long-term plans and focus on my immediate pleasure.

The rave was at an indoor waterpark called H2Oasis. I didn't come back out because, as ridiculous as raves are, I had never felt such a rush of acceptance and goodwill. There was no judgment, no shame, no blame. I took the occasion for freedom to wear a pink bandana and tight blue short shorts. I didn't need ecstasy or alcohol or even a joint to be with the crowd. I was all smiles. For the first time in my life, I was in a venue where the several men who noticed me could move closer. I danced with guys in public. Someone invited me to join his friends in a car wash, get high, and eat ice cream. I climbed in the backseat of a SUV to find a man so tall he had to hunch. He stared at me, his bright blue eyes growing wider.

"Oh my god, it's you," he said.

"Sorry?"

"You're the pink bandana boy."

I laughed. "It would appear so."

"You're like. Really, really cute."

I smirked. He was seven years older than me, a club promoter at night and worked in IT 9 to 5 for a bank. We kissed in the car wash, and dated till I left for college.

So the porn mags didn't sell, but I still felt compelled to use them, especially before Mom returned from the North Slope. I invited a couple of friends over who I knew wouldn't judge the dank apartment. We attempted to like beer, then watched the DVD in the back of the thicker magazines. The videos that twinkle in my memory are *40-Year-Old Anal Mamas* and *One in the Pink, One in the Stink*. We – a straight girl, a bi punk, then me – felt no arousal. We simply laughed, grateful that at 18 we were nearly finished with high school and finally free to consume smut from this great country. I spit up my beer at one frame in *One in the Pink, One in the Stink*.

"Is that Sadie Gruen?" I exclaimed, calling to memory a taller, big-boned girl with many freckles, always soft-spoken, coated in makeup. Her smile was always on, but had a low-watt, passive quality to it. One friend agreed it was her; the other dissented. We hold our respective views to this day. Sadie was wearing too much makeup for definitive identification.

Sadie. She's been a ridiculous figure for most of my life. But when I think of her now and consider that frail smile with small teeth all lined-up in a fine row, I feel her pain.

The only time a woman has unquestionably tried to have sex with me was at prom. To my horror and discomfort, it was my best friend, Jessica MacGuire.

It was around 2am, so the night was comparatively young, but we had been going hard since 2pm, when we

ditched sixth period and cracked open a couple of Four
Lokos in a Taco Bell parking lot. We suited up for prom
at her place. Her Mom took pictures of us right before
we left. We beamed all young and happy. I felt a strange
pride in being a plausible heterosexual male taking his girlfriend to prom.

Through middle and high schools, Jessica and I always
felt more comfortable dissenting from the crowd. Prom was
no different. Since I was on prom court, the school offered
to pay for a limo, but we passed. We'd rather spin around
in my mother's old Jeep Cherokee. We also passed on any
sit-down restaurant like Sullivan's Steakhouse or Orso's, and
elected McDonalds for dinner. We were pathetic rebels ever
since middle school band, when we had bonded over the
chemically disturbing ingredients in blue Powerade. As a
trombone player, I sat in the back near the percussionists,
where Jessica played the xylophone. We'd trade observations
about the brightness of our teacher's bald head, found ways
to imitate flatulence during a score's dramatic silence.

Jessica was my first friend in Alaska. We bonded quickly
over an eagerness to call bullshit. I loved how she arranged
Hot Topic chains, the seeming ease with which she abandoned the expectations placed on her, how — in her feeble
adolescent punk-ishness — she reveled in the forbidden. At
14, she listened patiently as I admitted, "I think I might be
bi," becoming the very first person to know my supposed
abnormality. A year later, I told a mutual friend that I had a
crush on Jessica; the response, returned to me through chan-
nels most indirect, was "Ew."

By 16, seemingly overnight, I was taller and leaner and
done with acne. Jessica now seemed to return the interest by slipping an envelope through the slits of my locker.
Inside were 20 colored photographs pressed together, each
sticky with fresh color ink. I tried to like these photos of
Jessica: close-ups of her hair, her straddling a bed in neon

green short shorts, blowing kisses, tracing her lips. I believe I ejaculated a couple of times to these images, the evidence of which has leavened the once smooth computer paper into a crinkly skin. But by 16, I was feeling affirmedly homosexual. I had already told Jessica about sucking a cock for the first time, getting fucked in the woods, bending over the hood for a closeted football player. She always asked for more details, about Mason, for instance, a handsome mixed-race kid I met through a district-wide Gay-Straight Alliance meeting, who later asked me to kick him in the balls at the Days Inn where he lived/worked; he had emancipated himself from his abusive parents at 15. Jessica, in turn, told me about getting a ring piercing somewhere around her vagina, and where those rug burns really came from. We'd laugh like hell and feel power in our vulgarity.

Of course, Abby and Victoria could never imagine how we spent our private time. They both always hoped that someday Jessica and I would become high school sweethearts. Grandma had hated Jessica at first, who dressed in all black with charcoal eyeshadow. "Why would that girl want to cover her beautiful body in all black?" Victoria asked. "Black is the color of Satan. And those piercings on her face, *mijo*, tell me why she has these ugly piercings on her face?" But once Jessica hit 15 and started wearing blues and purples and far less eye shadow, Grandma was all in. "Now when are you going to ask that nice girl on a date?" She'd ask. "She's beautiful. She won't be on the market forever. Grandson, do you remember when you were little you told me you wanted to have eight children?"

"Yes Grandma, I remember"

"Well, you got to start someday."

Mom was always fonder of Jessica, perhaps recognizing her talent, compassion, and that she simply was a teenage girl figuring herself out. "Sweet Jessica," Mom would ask at dinner. "How's our sweet Jessica doing these days?"

We were friends. Buds, really. And when she tried to kiss me after prom from the passenger seat of the Jeep, I flinched away and told her we (really just her) were still drunk, and should try to get some sleep.

Drunk, tired, embarrassed, or apathetic, Jessica didn't press on. We spent the next four hours sleeping reclined in our own seats. I drove her home before 8am, and we never talked about it.

Perhaps Jessica was surprised by her own attraction. By all accounts, I was a loser when we met, a bottom feeder in the social hierarchy of middle school. But by senior year, the butterfly was out. I was president of two clubs, lettering in tennis and debate. When most people look at my senior photo, the reaction is a variation of "Hot damn!"

The week leading up to prom, I was to wear a rented tux every day that the school had paid for. I still carried a proto-punk (or simply quasi) impulse to reject archaic social institutions like prom or homecoming. But in truth, I had never imagined myself on the receiving end of the glory. I liked that prom court got to skip class for lunches or field trips. I liked that our names were read over the loudspeaker, everyone suddenly spinning their heads in my direction with a newfound regard. I liked that the fee for prom was waived, that the court was ushered to the Bear Tooth one random afternoon for personal pizzas and unlimited root beer, all paid for by the PTA.

All this recognition made me feel what, looking back, I was always after: to feel special. I felt so special being on Prom Court that at times, I didn't follow through on my more radical plans, like jettisoning the school-appointed tux for a plain white tee and duct tape over my mouth to coincide with the Day of Silence, where students didn't speak for the day to protest the silencing of queer people. I still feel a lost opportunity there: to think, what a statement that would have made: someone on Prom Court is gay, someone worthy of recognition would not be here if certain groups got their way. But everyone, including the Gay-Straight Alliance advisor, told me to cut it out. "It's a great honor," the advisor told me. "You need to enjoy yourself. You're allowed to have a break."

Mom was, unsurprisingly, the biggest cheerleader to my upgraded status. Each day leading up to prom, I was to wear a slash over my tux where, in Grandma's favorite color, was printed *Prince Matthew*. Mom never let this go. For nearly a decade (how I wish we had reached another full decade) she'd greet me here and there, in person or text or email, with: *Love you beaucoup beaucoup, my Prince Matthew*.

Mom's interest in my actual prom night was such that she ended up inviting herself. And Caleb.

I'm still flabbergasted by this decision. Caleb had cheated on her. They were divorcing. She prayed each day to forgive him. Her anger at times terrified her. Once, watching him walk across the parking lot of Blackberry, Mom throttled the Jeep's engine, imagining the crack of his spine.

But now, here they were like the American Gothic couple, standing near the visitor's desk of The Anchorage Museum, awed by the spectacle of prom night, unsure of what to do next. My first reaction was outrage. How could she, I asked Mom, make this night all about herself. What other parents were there?

"There are chaperones!" she cried out, rightfully, if helplessly. Since I was eight, I felt a discomfort, for some reason I now regret, of seeing her at school, helping. By the fourth grade, I hid volunteer forms for the big bake sale; I intercepted requests in bright yellow or blue paper for after-school tutors. When she cried this chaperone observation, it wasn't over the unfairness that only certain parents could come to prom, but that I was barring her entry into my life.

It may have been, too, that her own prom was relatively awful. I lacked the decency to ever ask about Mom's prom, or my memory is too selfish to recall. It certainly couldn't compare to the museum of a fairly large city hosting 550 graduates. Caleb, I think, didn't attend his prom in Palmer. Mom tried to use this as justification for showing up unannounced.

I wish I had more patience to let them enjoy the spectacle. My mother often tried to improve her life through my own. I could resent this, the very last emotion she wanted to trigger. But I wish I had loved her incursions — all my pleas for boundaries and walls be damned.

When Mom and I overlapped at the same university, I once complained to a friend that Abby was essentially having me rewrite all her psychology papers. Software never became her forte. And something that remains my weakness is separating what people want from me versus what I think they need. Abby didn't ask me to rewrite her paper so much as help with formatting, but I happened to spot several areas for improvement. I figured she wanted deeper edits, but wouldn't explicitly ask for them. I was expecting some kind of sympathy from my friend, some commiseration at this inverted order of parent-child relations. Instead, I got these words to live by: "Matt. Do your Mom's damn homework."

I was 21 then and largely without wisdom. His bluntness was what I needed for my thick skull to do the sensible thing: help her. My willingness to help may have been motivated more by cringing over a potential slip up from an earnest lady I loved than a need to help on the individual's own terms. Perhaps I was too prideful to see that all she needed from me was rather simple. On some level, I wanted to believe that her problems were massive, and that what she required of me was burdensome and complex. Perhaps if that were the case, my disgruntlements with her and my situation would be justified.

Regardless.

I'm thankful that a clear-seeing, laconic voice came in

at some point to tell me to lower my ranking on the asshole Richter. To help my mother with her damn homework. To not recoil at the sight of her at "my" prom. I wish I had heard this voice sooner and, at 18, possessed the good sense to lead her to the dance floor.

CHAPTER 8

Country Roads

Once freshman year of college was up, the plan was to meet Mom in Chicago. From there, we'd drive to Potterville, Michigan, a town outside of Lansing. She had grown up there when the population sign read 900. The town had tripled since she left in the early 1980s. We were to visit her taciturn father and his second wife, Olga, a portly firecracker who filled his silence with cheerful talk of Spanish WWE and municipal news.

College had exhausted me. It wasn't only that the small campus meant everyone was in each other's business, or that a string of flings never resulted in the boyfriend I imagined. Those are typical inconveniences at any university. What overwhelmed me was the constant reminder that I could not afford to be here. It started with week-one orientation. A well-paid executive took to the stage with his allocated minute to say that each hour of class was around $410.

"Don't skip class," the lesson was. "Many of you have paid a lot for the privilege of being here. With every hour of class, your parents are paying $410. Don't waste it."

I followed the advice, and only signed up with professors at the top of their field. I took the most advanced courses I could, including a graduate seminar. I behaved as though Clark was a buffet and I should avoid the bread to fill up on the halibut.

My luck crashed with a course called "Ancient Cities." The renowned professor had a grant come through, so off he sailed for a dig in Turkey two days before class. His last-minute replacement was a newly minted Ph.D. who once read from the textbook for 12 minutes. As she mumbled about

Palmyra and struggled with a laser pointer, I questioned the value of a Clark education.

No matter how many notes I took, it was impossible to justify $410 per hour. I had changed for the better and still view my time there as foundational. But I also recall all the warning signs that I should have left after the first semester. I still hear one floor-mate from Bullock Hall saying she couldn't put her parents through another year of paying for an art degree.

"Like what am I even going to do with that?"

I started thinking this was wise. Mom's pleas to stay at Clark were losing their power. Especially around finances. "Do you even know all of the interest rates?" I raised my voice at her more than once. I ticked them off: 7.9%, 5.6%, 8.1%, subsidized, unsubsidized, forgivable or not. "And don't get me started on the private loans."

By late April 2009, I chose not to come back. What belongings I had collected freshman year I gave away. My peers said bye for the summer as I bid farewell to most of them for life. A couple of my close friends ran after the bus driving me toward the train station.

"We love you Alaska!" they shouted.

I had realized the movie-worthy freshman year with them: giggling high together, mattress-surfing downstairs, running from the cops at a basement party, analyzing boys ad nauseam. The bus driver laughed fondly. I put on sunglasses to hide my tears. I was a weird kid; Clark was a weird place; I had never so keenly felt that I belonged.

I planned on transferring to University of Arizona or UNC Chapel Hill. I was accepted to both in art history. But for some reason, I couldn't bring myself to go to an entirely new campus, find new friends; even when subsidized, it was cheaper to stay in Alaska. That summer after freshman year, I wasn't certain what the future held. I was just glad to go on a road trip with Mom.

She was too. When I returned to Alaska, Grandma's refrain became: "Oh *Mijo*. It sure is nice to have you back. She missed you so much. She sure did miss you." The weary sorrow in her voice — I knew it came from the accuracy of witness. I wondered how many hours the two had spent on the phone missing me.

College had cranked me open, in good ways and bad, always profound. Never had I met so many people from all walks of life. I learned that "St. Johns" usually meant a private school, that parents could miss Parents Weekend because they were vacationing in the south of France, that all the social striations that I encountered in movies were actually real; people like me were truly barred from that world — indeed, exclusion was what made the rich, rich. Someone called me out for saying "that's so gay"; I checked out a purple hardcover introducing me to queer theory; I learned of Michael Warner, Judith Butler, Leo Bersani, other gay historians like John D'Emilio and Jonathan Ned Katz. Someone was aghast when I didn't reject a plastic bag for a Monster energy drink from a gas station, a rejection I always knew made sense but never thought to enact; soon, I'd fall for the joke "You know you're a Clarkie when you're more concerned about recycling the beer can than getting caught." My first boyfriend, senior to my freshman, introduced me to cocktails. To this day, gin and tonics are my preferred drink, though none has tasted quite as fresh and expansive as the first he handed me.

I met people whose primary focus was truth rather than GPA. There was a premium on gathering knowledge for yourself, wielding it for your own good and the benefit of others. A fiery geography professor explicated globalization to an auditorium of 100 freshmen. The final project was to stand up in this room and give a speech for five minutes straight on any topic related to the course; oratory was dead, he said, but "I'm bringing it back." He asked if anyone wanted to try their skills now. My future friend Polly, a short-haired daughter of a Unitarian Universalist minister and brilliant lawyer, stood up. She was the figure of grace, confidence mastering nerves; she spoke flawlessly about changes to marine biology around New Zealand's coast. I told myself I could never do that, and withdrew.

Clark placed my ignorance and average intellect into sailing relief. A professor of neuroscience who liked to perform complicated equations in her head as a sort of magic trick to her captive audience gave me 53% on a group of midterm essays. It was 50% of the final grade. At the next class, she scratched the blackboard with the highest and lowest grades. 81% was the highest. I heard someone in the back say, "Whoa. Who got 53?"

I had been pretty good with humanities classes; I'd read the catalog multiple times for fun. Wanting to make the most of my $410/hour education, I signed up for a graduate seminar on contemporary British literature. My first presentation to that class remains my most epic failure. It stung doubly because I revered the audience: a Harvard graduate, two Fulbright students, graduate students who knew how to dress and carry themselves. I was an insecure freshman from Alaska who'd rather grow his hair long and neglected rather than handle the anxiety of small talk with a barber.

I took a "Law and Society" class meant for upperclassmen. Toward the end, in a group discussion on what we were taking away from the class, I said I considered myself a little bit of a Marxist now. "Is that like being half-pregnant?" the professor deadpanned. I was rather earnest and clueless. I can't fault her impatience.

But some professors valued my curiosity, creativity, and foolish ambition: professors of cognitive psychology and art history who were also disorganized and dreamy. My advisor happened to be a spirted Portuguese literature professor. She was the first to make majoring in English a possibility. I told her I could never be an English major. I got higher grades in other subjects, my sense of spelling was poor, my grammar too unwieldy, structure eluded me, I was no great orator like Polly.

"Oh please," she told me in the cramped Victorian house the English department called home. "You can learn all of that. What matters is your passion and what you observe."

I was tempted. I asked my quasi-boyfriend, a triple major in philosophy, English, and computer science, for advice. Everyone saw him as a genius. I wondered if he too got B+s on English papers freshman year. "All the time," he told me without shame. "More often Bs. But I wasn't really focused." His caveat of focus aside, their collective encouragement was enough for me to declare English literature as my major by the semester's end. That winter, I phoned my dad to say that I was gay. Another year would pass before I had the courage to tell him I was an English major.

I was 19 now, and Mom saw the new light in my eyes. It wasn't just youth, but the vibrancy that comes with doing what you want most in the world. The vivid life attained.

It's strange that I don't recall meeting Mom at O'Hare. This would be my first time in Chicago. Maybe I landed 12 hours early to do some solo exploring. Did we meet at the car rental office? Perhaps we were practical and took the train somewhere beyond the Beltway in search for cheaper car rentals.

In my mind, the trip really began once we left the Best Buy parking lot. It's strange: I don't recall if Mom joined me in the store or waited in the car. I know it was a sprint through; in no more than 10 minutes, I had found all the music we needed.

In Alaska, our music tastes were by and large circum-scribed by the inventory of strip malls. Anchorage, which was as spread out as a California suburb, didn't have record stores but row after row of CDs for purchase at Target and Walmart, each having passed the four Ps of marketing by the world's leading labels, everything designed for the heartland.

We found new artists at Barnes & Noble, Radio Shack, Sears. The one pure record store I knew of in Anchorage went belly up before I graduated high school in 2008.

In Southern California, Mom took me to the Barnes & Noble in Valencia, sandwiched between a Saturn deal-ership and a Baja "Mexican" restaurant. Through her guidance or my own nine-year-old curiosity, I wandered past the theft-detection devices humming like electric cen-turions, and into the rows of alphabetized CDs. It seemed like I discovered a new genre with each visit. How wild that you could demo any song for free. I must have spent hours punching in four-numbered combos to my favorites: Nichole Nordeman [Christian pop singer], Dixie Chicks [discovered through a babysitter who had a thing for "Earl Had to Die"], Faith Hill [her Maybelline commercials got me]. I liked Vivaldi, Goo Goo Dolls, No Doubt, The Roll-ing Stones, Everclear, Jewel, Whitney Houston, The Beatles, Alanis Morissette, Bach, and The Red Hot Chili Peppers.

During middle school in Alaska, we lived behind a shopping mall at 2200 Minerva Way. With nothing much to do in a one-bedroom dominated by the stank of Ca-leb's computer habits, I wandered through the aisles of Fred Meyer after school. I spent hours playing video games or finding new albums like "More Than You Think You Are" by Matchbox Twenty. For Abby, this may have been a wel-come evolution from the role models of yore — 98 Degrees, Backstreet Boys, O-Town, NSYNC. Matchbox Twenty was decidedly adult. They wrote about love, insecurity, betrayal, frustration, joy, disillusionment — topics I felt deeply but relied on others to articulate. While she was always happy to bop her head to boy bands, my sudden preference for Rob Thomas's soulful voice and caressed guitars must have been a memorable sign for Abby: her son was becoming a man.

We bought that album and listened to it throughout the summer of 2002. Corporate Fred Meyer picked up on our love, and added each track to its loudspeakers: "Unwell," "Disease," "Bright Lights," "All I Need," "You're So Real." When I went back to California, Mom heard Rob Thomas over the PA system and felt close to me. Years and years later, just driving by a Fred Meyer, she'd suddenly think of me, and hear each chord.

I purchased three albums from Best Buy for our summer drive to Michigan: Lady Gaga's "The Fame," "Show Your Bones" by the Yeah Yeah Yeahs, and the eponymous debut by Santigold. Most of these acts I heard in college, and while I likely would have stumbled on them eventually around the music section of Fred Meyer, it would have taken years. I seemed to have developed faster on the East Coast, and I was eager to share the fruits with Mom.

I don't recall the exterior of the rental car so much as the feeling inside, the buzz of being alive, and our readiness for adventure. First up was Gaga. I plopped it into the CD drive, which, unlike the Mustang, was sleekly built into the central console.

Out on the highway, the sky expanded for miles. We felt free and happy, flying toward Grandpa and his wife in Potterville. "Poker Face" was on repeat, Mom's hand playfully slapping the steering wheel, me explaining how she wrote this in ten minutes as a downtrodden student in a dank apartment in some neighborhood called the Lower East Side. Only years later would I put together that LES was the neighborhood of Santigold's lead single, "L.E.S. Artistes," and that Lady Gaga was hardly a struggling student, but the daughter of an upper-class businessman who paid for her private education at Manhattan's most elite school. As M.I.A commented on Lady Gaga's manufactured poverty, telling *Time Out London* in 2011: "[Lady Gaga's] journey isn't that difficult: to go from the fucking Upper East Side to a fucking performing arts school and onto a stage at the museum of fucking wherever. That journey's about four miles." Not that any of that would keep us from shouting "Poker Face" and "Paper Gangsta."

We loved the thrumming drive of "Say Aha" by Santigold, the ballroom baller beats of "I'm a Lady," the beach-run optimism of "You'll Find a Way." We were two people in the world's greatest amphitheater. Karen O singing "Dudley" and "Cheated Hearts," Mom nodding along to these new sounds, the sensibility and energy of my freshman year.

We didn't stay long in Michigan. We said hi to Grandpa, chair-bound in his living room. He and his wife seemed happy in their trailer park. He still kept a cane on one side of his blue La-Z-Boy, then a stretchable "claw arm" to his right, which I had last seen a decade ago at eight. Now a man, my conversation with him was stilted. It seemed that Mom ran into the same loveable wall: she wanted a deeper connection that he simply could not provide. He had always been a quiet, slow-moving man. Dependable, which is why Grandma married him after two previous marriages. My father's side of the family liked him for never putting on "airs" and causing trouble, unlike Grandma, who, when she wasn't shaving her head, wore feathered church hats, sombreros, or brightly-colored pillbox hats. But I never felt close to him. Perhaps that would've changed had I known something about baseball or basketball. Mom may have felt the same. She loved her father, but their relationship was more complicated than I would ever know. I caught glimpses of their quiet pain and stilted love. Anything more in-depth, imagination constructs.

We visited my Uncle Jim and Aunt Stephanie. I'd like to portray them in a humorous vein, but unlike Grandma, their "crazy" was unempowering. None of it was self-selected. Jim, at 16 or 17, was in a car accident that nearly left him dead. His brain so severely inflamed that he never fully recovered. He'd spend the remaining decades with a glass eye and the mind of an immature prankster, calling into radio stations in caricatured voices, or sending in mixed tapes as a resume to prove he could DJ.

Uncle Jim married a large black woman named Stephanie. She had schizophrenia and often refused to take her meds. Her family was well off and high-functioning; they supported her, but had to keep her at a distance. It saddens me now to think all they could do was send her money; they'd already learned that to emotionally invest in Stephanie would drag them under without helping her.

I have a photo of Stephanie. It's a cruel photo: she's jerking her neck to look back at something, the sky behind her is dramatic and wild, rumbling up a storm; there's a dumpster tucked in the corner, comically dwarfed by her gigantic breasts jutting out in a brown tight-tee shirt; her face is in a frantic cast, all her impulses scattered. The drama of her bewilderment was fit for Jacques-Louis David. I showed it to Mom. I know now that we laughed so not to cry.

Stephanie stopped taking her medicine when we were there. She, like Jim, played games with people. I recall raised voices from Stephanie, Mom's indefatigable patience, the repeated warnings, "You need to take your medicine, Steph. Or I will have to call your case manager. And I'll do it. You know I will." I recall her sympathy for Stephanie. And Stephanie, sensing that a real person wanted to see her as a real person, bore herself to Abby. The shield of her playfulness weakened. In pieces, she showed herself to Abby. I heard the sorrow in Stephanie's voice. "They make me sleepy," she told Abby. "They make me fat. They make me funny."

Mom, as she did so well with countless people, listened. In her presence, her unguarded and undivided attention, people became real. After hours of back and forth, Stephanie finally took the pills.

The rest of the trip was pleasant enough. We visited Mom's best childhood friend, Joy, who owned three ferrets, had a young son living with his father for the summer, had just filed for bankruptcy, and had never left the state of Michigan. They made a fun pair growing up: Joy, the flirt in short skirts and diaphanous blouses; Mom, dressed like a preacher's daughter, her long brown hair flowing past her bum. Joy took us out to eat at an American restaurant with steel benches inside, covered by glossy picnic cloth of red, white, and blue. A woman, I forget if it was Joy or one of her friends, asked if I had a girlfriend.

"I'm not really interested right now," I replied. "I'm too busy."

I recall the knowing smile. "Oh. That will change."

We passed through the quiet side streets, the mellow hills up and down.

"This place has changed a lot," Mom told me, "and hardly at all."

We passed her high school. She was salutatorian in a graduating class of 15.

What I most remember about the trip was getting out. I think Abby, too, was grateful to leave. She never felt she could spread her wings in Potterville. From the few characters I had met, I understood why Abby had to get out. I, too, couldn't see myself becoming who I wanted to be anywhere near Potterville.

The ride back was happy, but not as ebullient as the ride coming to, when we didn't know precisely what would happen. We were tired. Weighed down, perhaps, with all our new knowledge of our Michigan kin. We wanted a day for ourselves and rest from fatigue. We stopped in a town named Chestnut. I forget which state it was in, but the town was all allure: the leaves, the quaint library, the row of stores down main street. Years later, I'd learn that chestnut trees once filled every block of America; they were as common as pines. But then a plague came just for chestnut trees, traveling on in from Europe. They're all dead now, or practically extinct in North America. But the town remains *Chestnut*; as do the hundreds of other towns across America that took their name from their cherished surroundings. We liked the town of *Chestnut* because it felt so American, of the apple pie variety that we always wanted to consume, but that always remained distant because, like most Americans, we had no knife.

CHAPTER 9

Midnight Sun Espresso

I've probably had better coffee than what's served in Anchorage. But it doesn't feel that way. Nothing can quite compare to the crispness of a mocha made by Kaladi Brothers on Northern Lights Boulevard, or the strength of an Americano from Steamdot on Benson. In terms of black coffee, Raven's Brew clears my head like no other. But my judgments are skewed. How could I not be partial toward Alaskan roasts? I shared thousands of cups of coffee with Abby.

Shortly after moving to Alaska, cafes became a shelter for us. In 2002, walking around downtown Anchorage when the snow became too fierce and the cold had penetrated too deeply through the Mustang's blanket "window," we ventured inside Dark Horse Coffee on F Street. The barista owner welcomed our shivering forms. The couches were pleasing to sight and touch, the walls orange and lively. We played "Guess Who" for nearly an hour, laughing over hot chocolate as we made up stories behind the faces we were about to knock flat. The hot chocolate comforted us. We exchanged knowing smiles, as if we discovered something special in this strange, new land.

One of Mom's first jobs in Alaska was as a dishwasher in Palmer's Vagabond Blues Cafe. She was desperate for money. She didn't want to take much from Dad, so she settled for a sliver of the Mums Drive house sale, and the $3,000 profit for the Sonoma truck we had crossed the country with listening to Whitney Houston. That money wasn't enough to establish a new life in Alaska, especially for someone like Mom, who never was adept at managing money. She liked the warmth of Vagabond Blues, so similar to Dark Horse with its community vibe and bright pastels. There were knitted caps for sale and a 20-foot-map of the world. I joined her for work most days. The staff gave me unlimited cups of hot cocoa. I'd sit in the corner reading comic strips as the sun came up. I smiled at a couple of the early morning regulars, including a man about 70 named Donald, who liked to tease me about waiting for my girlfriend. By 10:30am, my fellow 11-year-old, Peter, who was also homeschooled, walked into Vagabond with his Mom for an early school break. Peter and I played chess and talked about which movie we watched last night. I tended to make bad moves to make the game last longer.

By noon, the lunch rush made it difficult to focus. I'd walk around what I dubbed downtown Palmer: I'd check Grandma's PO Box or visit a used bookstore called Fireside. If I was really cut out for a walk, I'd jog across the Glenn Highway to the grocery store, Carrs, and look at scattered toys, books, and magazines; they had the best sesame chicken, where hours under a heat lamp solidified its lumpy goodness. Other days, I'd travel across the inoperable railroad tracks to the petite Palmer Public Library.

I can't answer if Mom was worried about my globe-trotting. I think she trusted me to be safe. I had a cheap Nokia phone. If a true emergency ever did greet me, I could easily call her or the police. She had learned from her own restrictive childhood not to hold people from the world. Some of her favorite characters were Huckleberry Finn and Tom Sawyer. She'd likely nod along to that declaration attributed to Twain: "I have never let my schooling interfere with my education." She would do everything in her power to protect me from mortal harm, but she wasn't going to hamper my explorations, even as securing my safety would have settled her nerves.

I've often wondered why, when, and how my love of coffee began. Looking back, it's obvious that it began here, with Mom at these two cafes. But in college, I recall thinking about the origins of my coffee habit, how in high school I'd rather serve detention for tardiness than miss some form of espresso. There were days I counted out 210 pennies for the PTA moms who controlled the high school's cafe. In thinking back to when this want became a need, I thought (of all people) about Michael Cera.

In 2007, Cera was peaking with movies like *Superbad* (released in August) and *Juno* (September). Some teachers and friends started saying I looked or acted like him. I perceived this as both compliment and insult. But seeing Michael Cera praised on the big screen – an awkward, anxious, soft-spoken boy like me – gave me hope that I could one day become as special and lauded as I silently dreamed and craved. When I hustled around school with a few textbooks in one hand, a Styrofoam cup in the other, I imagined myself being some Michael Cera character – potentially weird, but loved in the end for such oddities. Perhaps I needed to be seen around school holding a cup of coffee because it had become essential to this image I softly wanted.

I imagined making myself so different from my origins, from my family. A sophomore writing assignment in high school had me write about family similarities and differences. I wrote a page or two of dialogue imitating my father. I emailed it to myself, but accidentally sent it to him (we share the same initials). I followed up with a frantic email saying this was all fiction, and I didn't mean any of it; it didn't even sound like him. To my shock, Dad replied, "No, sounds like me." It shocked me that he could see this unflattering portrait of himself, yet be satisfied with changing none of his behavior.

At 16, I became convinced that I was different from my father and sister, even Mom. It was a fact I feared, yet embraced. I read *The Mysteries of Pittsburgh* at 19 and fell for Arthur, a suave, gay 19-year-old I secretly hoped to model myself after. I was so awed that he could reach a point where no one could have imagined that he, the son of a maid, had originated without any of the advantages that now appeared to be his birthright. In thinking for years that I held coffee cups around campus to be like Michael Cera, I supported this theory that I was in the process of making a *sui generis* persona. But Mom, like so much else, had built the foundations by taking me to cafes. She was entirely unlike my father, who always took his coffee through drive-throughs; she stayed to enjoy the life inside. This simple habit was everything. It taught me to talk to people, to take the time to involve myself in the intellectual and social life of my surroundings. Café culture has altered, if not determined, intellectual and political history, as Mark Pendergrast documents in *Uncommon Grounds: The History of Coffee and How It Transformed the World*. Once Ben Franklin and company switched afternoon gin for coffee, they could (naturally enough) formulate and share ideas that shaped the world. In my own world, that's what Mom did to me. Her openness to everything, to everyone, was vital to who I'd become. She was the prism through which light became color. If I may think that I discovered and deepened my love of coffee by myself, it's indisputable that Mom led me to the cafe. I did become someone radically different and better than my background, but I did not, even as the congratulations would serve my ego, do it alone.

At 45, Mom returned to nursing school, something she had nearly finished in California. I was a junior in high school, and between our academic schedules, we developed a fondness for Midnight Sun Espresso every morning. We loved driving by the bright yellow coffee kiosk, especially in the a.m. when they gave us a free copy of *The Anchorage Daily News*. The owner lived near us. Whenever she was in, she'd tell the baristas to make our drinks free. Our preferred drink was the marshmallow mocha – "Just heavenly" – Abby would say after every other sip. They placed a chocolate-covered coffee bean on the lip of all our paper mugs. If we didn't have the right change (common. Neither of us planned much) the kiosk took IOUs.

That last part fascinated everyone from out of state. When Victoria was diagnosed with colon cancer in 2016, I flew up from New York with my boyfriend, Adam. He had bonded with Abby and Victoria from previous visits. Victoria liked that he was tall and "one of God's chosen people." Abby liked that she could pleasantly talk with him for hours. Everything about Anchorage fascinated Adam, especially the litany of coffee kiosks around town. He had grown up in Pennsylvania where people grabbed cheap coffee from a gas station, or took a 30-minute coffee break at a diner. The East Coast generally has more going on than Alaska, but when it comes to coffee, it lacks the incentive to develop rich networks for caffeine intake. Coffee was essential to making some sense of time under a midnight sun. The need for coffee in Alaska was so well-understood and honored that Midnight Sun Espresso was hardly the only kiosk around town to honor the IOU.

As Victoria endured various doctor appointments, I recall driving across town once just to take Adam to Midnight Sun Espresso. We ordered, and I had totally blanked that they didn't accept cards. The cheerful barista told us not to worry, just come back later with cash.

"Wow," Adam said, pulling away in the rented Lexus. "That was nice of them. That'd never happen in New York." I was suddenly proud of the place I came from. Having lived in Manhattan for years, I was realizing this trust in people was atypical for much of America.

I wonder why Mom wasn't with us on this trip. Likely, she was caring for her own mother. Perhaps we were bringing her a mocha. Perhaps I taped the lid, or asked for one of those plastic stickers that covered the lid — all happy shapes like frogs with rouge cheeks or skipping giraffes, winking stars or full moons with fat grins — those stickers Mom and I used to decorate our binders or the dashboards of our current car. Perhaps I gave her this mocha in the lobby of Captain Cook Hotel, where Grandma insisted on staying a couple of nights before she left Alaska for San Diego, where she would pass. Perhaps Mom clasped this yellow cup, warm and familiar, giving me a side hug, taking one sip of the elixir, before turning to me, a hand dramatically placed over her heart, her eyes widening, her voice a stage whisper:

"My *Word* ! Matthew. This is simply heavenly."

CHAPTER 10

Talkeetna

In my memory, my family took two road trips across the country. The first was to Wisconsin to see my father's family. I rode a three-wheeler for the first time and burned my right thigh on the carburetor; Lee Ann and I had been fixed on the curious process of two mosquitoes mating when my dad's youngest brother swatted the pair to death.

"What you do that for," Lee Ann cried.

"Because love stinks," he replied.

My father slapped me in the face hard as he could to make me stop crying; I played soccer with cousins who were nicer than the judgmental ones in Texas; a kind aunt introduced me to her craft table and she taught me how to make dream catchers and when she died of breast cancer years later, I cried for a week, even though I had only hung out with her that one day in 1998.

The happier road trip occurred a year before. It was just my sister, me, and Mom. We were to see Mom's dad in Michigan. He lived in the same trailer park I'd see again when I was a 19-year-old in college. That was the first time I saw fireflies. They pulsated from the wet lawns of Michigan; a radical contrast to the gritty brown backyards of our Southern California. I heard my first ghost story there. The neighborhood kids gathered around to hear of a guy who got decapitated – precisely how was irrelevant – so he spent his midnight hours stalking neighborhoods, luring the innocent into dark corners to make them look like himself, i.e., headless. I think back to a film interpretation class at The University of Alaska Anchorage with a jittery adjunct whose verbal ticks included "in regards to" and "the ways in which" and "in terms of" telling the class how the horror genre hinges on a violent, usually unasked for transformation — almost always into something radically different from the original, something "foreign" or "ugly." Of course, I didn't think this ghost story was trying to prepare me for a lifetime of mistrusting strangers. But it was. The ghost stories of lower-class children, I wonder if they differ from their wealthier peers, from the families that tame villains through job offers.

We rode in a petite black GMC Sonoma. I sat on one of the two back seats in the rear cabin that folded out to face each other like paddy wagon benches. The cramped quarters weren't a problem for me at the time. I rather appreciated the smart use of space, and never complained of my confinement.

I don't recall the trip beginning until we left California. In Arizona, I asked to see the Grand Canyon. Mom said we could on the way back (We didn't. I forget the rationale.) We passed through Oklahoma: immensely open skies and abundant cornfields. Having repeatedly seen the tornado-chasing movie *Twister* (1996), I was terrified that a tornado would touch down at any second and suck up our tiny truck, throwing us around like I did to matchbox cars, deaf to the passenger screams inside.

The clearest memory is of Whitney Houston. *The Preacher's Wife* (also 1996) stared Whitney and Denzel Washington. Mom wasted no time in buying it on VHS. We loved everything about that movie: the singing, the clapping, the smiles and love. Love conquered all in *The Preacher's Wife*. The innocent triumphed. Pernicious real estate agents were exposed to be feeble-spined weaklings, cast down to their knees by the forces of Righteousness. We re-imaged the joy of that movie in our tiny car, free from the bounds of a staid suburb.

"Step by Step" was our favorite. Followed by "I Go to the Rock" and "Hold on Help Is on the Way." It strikes me these are all anthems for the downtrodden, or for people who want to be good, who never believe that their work on planet Earth is ever entirely done. The songs are clarion calls to keep going. They assume hardship and a certain un-happiness. That Mom and I resonated with this music seems elucidating. I cannot speak for my sister.

Or my half-sister. At 19, Mom told me she had a one-night stand with a German bloke on a beach in Virginia. About a month later, she met my dad. She told him in tears a few weeks later. He was so smitten with her then that he said he didn't care; they'd raise the kid as his. In this regard, he was always good to his word. My father was a different man when young.

Lee Ann is technically my half-sister, but it feels like a cheap shot to call her that. We grew up together. She was the first to inform me about sex and sexuality. We built cas-tles together out of our comforter, or "Afghans." She was four years older than me but was willing to play "War" with my Aladdin figurines. She laughed when I pretended to be at Santa Ana, the apostolic megachurch; I'd sprint around the house beating my head against the wall or thrashing my body on Mom and Dad's bed until I dizzied. It saddens me to know I only caught her attention when I was mean to others or hurting myself.

Lee Ann drove me to middle school when I lived with her and Dad in SoCal. I saw her indifference to others as a sign of strength. When her best friend flipped her off in fare-well, I figured that was the ultimate sign of cool. But by the time I was in 8th grade and she was a senior in high school, I was accepting this unnerving fact: my sister was hardly cool. What I had seen as robust apathy was the cover for her fundamental insecurity, which had a self-promulgating, hermeneutic quality, like a convection current whose surface is by turns amputated sensitivity and extreme selfishness. She was callous, petty, and paranoid that anyone would think themselves better than she. She hung out with similarly judgmental people. This included Tiffany, the best friend whom she constantly found fault with, and her boyfriend, Ryan, whose dream job was to be co-host of *Jackass* and whom she routinely called stupid. Her worst traits came out in awful relief the week our mother died. Perhaps tragedies, like a parent's death, push us to reveal our most elemental qualities. Hers were sinister. I never quite believed in evil until I saw how she behaved.

I haven't spoken to her since she left Abby's deathbed, but to call her my half-sister, as enticing as that is, rings false. She did me wrong. She did Mom wrong. But she is still my sister, however different we will always be.

I love that Whitney Houston highlights our differences. Lee Ann liked Whitney, but Mom and I adored her. Lee Ann was drawn to handsome, stolid white guys with deep voices who could belt: Incubus, Chris Cornell, Hoobastank, Goo Goo Dolls, The Calling. They sang of love with uncommon mundanity. Most of their lyrics are about changing oneself for the beloved ("The Reason"), waiting for the beloved to love them ("Like a Stone"), following them no matter what ("Wherever You Will Go"), or being understood only by them ("Iris"). I love some of these songs, but I see that all of them have an us–against–the–world quality. They're about raising walls. They're insular. They're passive. They're presumptive of love.

The tracks we blared from *The Preacher's Wife* soundtrack were all about breaking down walls, energizing the audience to reach out to others and find the power to love. The songs presumed thankfulness for a higher power. They thought love was possible, but required action, loyalty, effort.

It bothered me, perhaps unfairly, that my sister played depressing pop-rock in the hospital where our mother laid nonverbal. Abby couldn't move either. The last thing I heard her say, with great effort, was "luf you." She could die at any moment, and Lee Ann had demanded I pick her up at the airport, as she never called ride shares in California and didn't want to deal with a taxi in Anchorage. We fought, me saying I didn't want to leave Mom, she saying she didn't sign up for this and that I was reneging on a promise. To shut her up, I sped over to the airport.

By 2017, Abby had been re-married for several years to a gentle, slightly dopey man named Jeremy. He was the sort of God-fearing man she had seen in Caleb, but was far kinder; this time she was only a decade older, not two. Jeremy watched Abby as I sped to the airport to make peace with Lee Ann. He said he'd call as soon as anything appeared wrong. I picked Lee Ann up from Ted Stevens International Airport. We hugged and went for breakfast like nothing was wrong.

Back at the hospital, I talked with the hospice staff in the hallway. When I came back, Lee Ann stood at the foot of Mom's hospital bed, the objects of her purse placed around Mom's covered feet, a trail of brushes, makeup, and tampons were between and around her legs; Lee Ann actually considered it as good a site as any to rearrange her purse. She had brought a portable Sonos speaker to blast "Dani Girl" by Red Hot Chili Peppers, Lee Ann's favorite lyric being one she felt described herself: "She's a runner/ rebel and a stunner." That she shut off the music I knew Mom loved – Darlene Zschech, Chopin, Faith Hill – for music that uplifted only her own healthy body, infuriated me. In nearly every memory I have of Lee Ann, she was only thinking of herself.

She was chewing gum as I watched her from the doorframe. She held her phone lackadaisically from the wrist, as if bored and thinking about her next Instagram selfie. I hated her in that moment. I hated this girl who had always been selfish and untrusting, a leech for attention and power, who became an officer in the LAPD where people, no matter how richer or better looking or skilled, would have to pay attention to her and do what she commanded.

I couldn't tolerate this woman who was fighting me not to move Mom to hospice, thus ignoring Abby's wish to pass at home. I still have trouble believing that Lee Ann suggested cremation over burial, despite Abby's wishes, because it was cheaper; that she only made time to see Mom twice in the year before her death — both short trips; she did not pay for the funeral or any of Abby's plane tickets; Lee Ann was against modern medicine and convinced Mom to try a "natural" diet that shortened her prognosis from two or three years to less than one; who was not around to make the disgusting green protein shakes she had sent to a UPS store, where I picked them up after a tense conversation with a clerk: ("Why can't the recipient pick it up herself" "She's ill and is too tired." "Can she come in later?" "She has cancer." The clerk called over her manager. "Barb, this man's mother allegedly has cancer and can't sign for the package, what do we do?"). My sister was not there to care for Mom in her last month. She did not see her become too weak to twist off a cap for water, or trip on the slight step for a handicap ramp, vomit from the passenger seat, nearly wreck the car when she insisted on driving back from chemo. My sister was not there to see Mom staring at a white wall, considering what she had achieved and the considerable hopes finally concluding. My sister did not hear the doctor a week before saying "The truth is she's dying," or find Abby collapsed on the floor. My sister did not call the fire department because she could not get her fallen mother upright and into bed without hurting her. My sister did not look into her dying eyes filling with black toxins, hear her rasped breathing, hold her hand as the warmth receded, or hear her breathing suddenly stop.

In the hospital room, I asked Lee Ann to play something softer. She glared at me, and snarled, "What's your problem?"

But Mom taught me to find joy in everything, even in the terrible; find and emphasize the truly great. Believe you can turn awful realities around.

One of the happiest road trips of my life was to Fairbanks, Alaska. Lee Ann was with me and Mom for the summer. I believe it was 2003, but it may have been the year prior; I'll go with 2003. Lee Ann was 17, and at 13, I was officially living with Mom. The distance helped my sister and me get along. And with age, we simply had more to talk about: Harry Potter, The Dixie Chicks, "the war on terror."

We drove off in the Mustang from South Anchorage. It must have been June. I was coming out of a quasi-goth phase where I wore head-to-toe black, baggy rayon pants, unfunctional zippers, spiked up all my hair. Photos from this trip show what I considered to be a summer shirt: a white t-shirt with grey sleeves, "No Fear" printed across the sternum, and a skull at the center. I brought a couple of toys with me that we all took turns playing with: a pink disc spinner that spiraled discs up 20 feet; a Nerf blaster that shot out vibrantly colored doilies. Lee Ann was happy enough to sing with us in the car. She possessed a never-before-seen maturity not to disparage everything about Alaska and repeat how much she preferred Cali. Mom, of course, was ecstatic to have her two babies so close. I am astounded how her optimism never ceased.

My favorite stop on that trip was Talkeetna, about 70 miles north of Wasilla. The population's ebb and flow fascinated me: 3,000 people in the summer, fewer than 1,000 by winter. We walked along the railroad to find multi-tiered forests, jagged rocks spearing out, paddle-sized leaves everywhere because of the summer's universal sun. We all were, having spent decades in the armpit of California, astonished by the green surroundings, the fresh rivers, mountains unobstructed. None of us could articulate this wonder. Mom got closest with a chorus of, "It's all so beautiful."

I don't recall what we talked about. Probably gentle memories we all shared, like the time Lee Ann's angry cockatiel, Tony, chased one of her friends around the house for a solid minute, or the time our rabbit in California, Katie, who somehow became very spiteful against the world, nearly swiped the pinkie off a neighborhood bully who tried poking her through the cage, or the time the pastor's son died in a car crash and Mom left a long voice message that was to serve as a substitute for her absence at the funeral. She concluded her heartfelt memory of the young man with "We all love you. So yes. Well, I hope you have a good day anyway." She cringed before returning the phone to its cradle, knowing she would now have to drive to the young man's burial.

The three of us were happiest when turning slapstick. We had so thoroughly explored Talkeetna that Mom decided to splurge on a cheap motel there. A photo from one of her disposable cameras reminds me that Lee Ann enacted some of our favorite characters: a woman who dunked her head in a pool of water, flipped the density over her face to look like Samara from *The Ring*. Then she'd suddenly wag her finger and in a high-pitched Mary Poppins lilt, intone: "No Talking in the Library! There Will Be No Talking in the Library!" Another photo shows Lee Ann peeking past a shower curtain, her face sparkling with mischief, all her hair stretched back in a bun to support her rousing rendition of "Matchmaker, Matchmaker." We were all having too much fun rekindling memories together that we went to bed long past midnight.

The next day, we had breakfast in the hotel (or lunch, if we slept in and Mom finagled a late check out). Mom asked someone to take a photo of the three of us.

We sat in front of an unlit fireplace surrounded by the picturesque: old Alaska license plates, folded American flags in memorial containers, wood logs framing black and white photos of Old Talkeetna. It remains my favorite photo from that trip: Mom's in the middle, her lips are unusually red, less by makeup than, I think, freedom: a stronger connection to nature, a reunion with the beings she loved most. Maybe it's the white shirt she's wearing with the equally red logo for Polo Jeans across her breasts that makes her face stand out as if chiseled. She is early 40s. Young, able-bodied, grateful in the photo, yet aware of all she stands to lose, that the presence of her two children together may not last. Lee Ann and I, neither of us sense this. We lean into our mother's open arms and feel her warmth as we nuzzle closer. Neither of us sense the wariness in our mother. Neither of us could imagine she'd one day be gone, and there'd be nothing left holding us together.

CHAPTER 11
Blood Type

Around 2010, we drove everywhere around Anchorage.

I was 20. She was 47.

I had wound up where I least wanted to be: The University of Alaska. Abby worked for the Salvation Army, counseling people with drinking problems. She liked it but wanted to finish her bachelors to take on a more active role during group therapies. We shared a studio on I Street in downtown Anchorage. It was far better than the Spenard one, but I still felt like a failure for living with my mother. I tried asserting some independence by turning the closet with its slanting ceiling into my own dimly-lit room. I slept on a cot my grandmother's friend didn't want. Every day, I woke up resentful and brittle for being a loser who couldn't make his dreams real. The most trivial thing could set me off.

Once driving through downtown, I responded to one of her gentle requests, which I read as intrusive, with a typhoon of cruelty. I forget what I said, or what we were even talking about, but it was the first time she showed vulnerability. From my peripheral view, I knew I had hurt her. She shuddered, "Why do you have to be so nasty."

The moment was rare enough to shock me out of my assholery. I apologized. She forgave me. Cycles like this repeated for months. Something inconsequential and meant with the best of intentions was met by me with callous clapbacks. I'd ask for her forgiveness; she'd forgive me; then I'd resent her for putting me in positions where I had to apologize, which triggered further anger that I could not accept my mother for who she was. More anger still that she so easily forgave — as though she could not defend herself. I was disappointed and angry with myself that I could not love my mother for all that she was, and that I could not accept with grace the fact that where you come from influences if not determines who you are. She loved me absolutely, and I was too embarrassed and ashamed and malcontented to do the same. Her acceptance challenged me every day to accept myself. I couldn't do that in my early 20s, so I latched on to her infinite kindness and bit down hard, like a snake that couldn't unclench its jaw until all of the venom had run out.

I hated when she said I was like my father.

"Some of your mannerisms," she'd tell me slowly, as if she were working through the amazement herself, "are just like his." It was an observation. Not a compliment or judgment. But the pairing of father and son jarred me.

My father and I, our mannerisms can betray an everyday impatience with the world. They demonstrate insecurity with a need to get away from people fast, to brag, to cut down others acerbically. It's simple stuff: taking two steps at a time after a concert, judging people's weight and perceived intelligence, weaving impatiently in and out of traffic, holding the head upright like a royal dancer. There are cadences within me that echo him: they appear when I speak to strangers, when I pose happier than I am to win people over, consciously constructing myself as a personable persona with all the studied yet seamless moves of a surgeon. The mannerisms I inherited from my father are "nasty." Since my early 20s, I have deliberately attempted to unlearn them.

But Mom noted more than once that I am my father's blood type.

This is not to say that all of Mom's mannerisms and habits of mind were unquestionably good. She tended to perform outsized displays of emotion, surprises at mundane occurrences that were meant to foster interest and goodwill in whoever she met. I disliked seeing her like this; I thought she was acting like a puppet. But to live in this world, we must oblige and intrude and manipulate more or less constantly. This was a kinder form of manipulation, I think, than Dad's dark humor. But the relative detestability of either approach is dwarfed in sadness by the fact we all are reduced to such a mixture of ignoble tactics in this enterprise known as sociability.

But Mom's genuine, if outsized, delight at the seemingly small was as real as Dad's massive irritability. Perhaps genuine is the wrong word. What's hard for me to understand is how someone can be so delighted with the world. Pure. Nothing underhanded, no agenda, honest to a fault; qualities that won't get you ahead in a world ruled by concealment. Was I frustrated that she wouldn't play by crueler, harder-driving rules? Perhaps a part of me resented her for being living proof that I was adjusting too well to the world's fouler qualities.

Both my parents could have temperamental flare-ups, but Mom's tended to be more dramatic (and entertaining). One story I've told through the years coincides with that family road trip in 1998. From California to Wisconsin, we were to meet Dad's family outside of Madison, sleeping each night in a trailer he hitched to the ruby-red Oldsmobile Bravada he once loved. We were looking for a campground near Mount Rushmore. It was nearing 3am. We were exhausted, but Mom, worn down by Dad's swipes at her navigational abilities, was at wits' end. Dad told her to take a turn.

She missed it. His comment was something to the effect of *Good one, Abby*.

She slammed the breaks. The dogs yelped. I had been in and out of consciousness, but now the seatbelt strung me tight.

She yelled, "I can't take it anymore!!" and got out of the car.

She barreled down the empty road, lit only by the funnel of the SUV's headlights. I still see her running away, her long black hair flowing, threadbare and illuminated, then swallowed in the dark.

Half a minute passed. Lee Ann and I looked on in shock from the backseat. Lee Ann spoke first: "Is she coming back?"

My father waited several beats. "She'll be back."

A couple of minutes later, she was walking back with her palms crossed to hold the opposite elbow.

"I'm sorry guys," she said soon as she opened the door. "I don't know what got into me."

I don't recall Dad apologizing for being a habitual jerk. I cannot recall him apologizing. Not once in his entire life.

Mom tried to laugh her explosion off. We let her.

That afternoon, all was forgiven, if not forgotten. For years, Lee Ann and I laughed about the time our long-haired Good Christian Mother lost her shit. We saw humor in the story, perhaps because we could not handle the fact she was trapped. We could not see the necessity of her declaration — *I can't take it anymore* — nor could we handle its immediate implication that our family was ending.

CHAPTER 12

Sonnet 73

Mom loved Jane Vaughan. Jane became my roommate at 21, and remains one of my most talented and least accomplished friends. I loved her devil-may-care attitude to the world: she was here to make money, drink and dance, rock out on the keyboard, and die. She dyed her hair a magma color that Victoria would have applauded had Jane concealed her 12 tattoos or wisps of a lacey black bra. Jane introduced me to her friends — Julian, a guy who could only cum to porn after three hours, and whose bi-curiosity I once entertained; Jane's boyfriend, Anish, who I first met after she sent him to pick me up for a party and who, minutes after dropping me off, was peeing in the kitchen sink to prove to everyone's wide eyes that his dick was indeed wide as a beer can; I met Roger, the perpetually kind, white skier-bro, and Rayne, a cocky bombshell not unlike Raquel Welch, who enjoyed Roger's hopeless love. They were seen passed out in several bathtubs around town, but Rayne made it clear to all with ears that she would never actually *sleep* with Roger. I watched Roger respond to this once in a kitchen. He nodded, took a sip of beer, and stared at the ceiling.

Around these people I was in constant drunken debauchery, and Jane Vaughan was our ring leader. Take the Naughty Nurses and Dirty Doctors party. Jane took me as her +1. It was a house party where I solidified my love of vanilla vodka. I appeared in scrubs and a tight white-tee. Jane wore a black corset, rubbery nurse's hat, and a black leather whip she had turned into a stethoscope. She took three steps inside and was swept up by admirers. I told her to go on without me. I usually had no trouble chatting people up at parties, especially with my wingman Booze. But at this party full of breeders, in a crowded house where you had to shout to be heard, I couldn't connect with anyone beyond an awkward *Hey*. Thirty minutes passed, and I was feeling dazedly alone. But I wanted to feel happy with all these people. I wanted to bond, be sociable and fun. To submerge the disagreeable misery holding me back, I drank.

Within an hour, I had taken 13 shots of vanilla vodka, along with the beers I had consumed whenever I understood the mob to be cheering. I last recall running out in the lawn barefoot with two strangers, running outside like kids released for recess, best friends for the moment. I recall spinning in the center of a road. My hands were spread out far and wide like Jesus the Redeemer. I spun faster and faster into happy oblivion.

It worked.

Dimly, there was consciousness on the host's couch. I was in someone else's purple shirt. A male voice joked that I sure could eat a lot of Chinese food. I passed out again.

Jane prodded me in front of Mom's apartment. "Hey Matt. We're at your Mom's place. Do you think you can walk with just me helping, or should I call her?"

I don't know if I replied. At some point, Mom burst out of the apartment. She was in a turquoise robe and barefoot. It's telling that I remember her rushing toward me, but I don't recall the exact mechanics of how she helped me, how she nursed me back to health. With her presence assured, I was safe to roll back into unconsciousness.

But then I recall some consternation. Mom, in her haste, had locked herself out of the apartment.

Luckily, Jane Vaughan was nothing if not resourceful. The studio lay on the ground floor. The large living room window was accessible from the street. Jane, in her eight-inch heels and black corset, stepped through the hyacinths and tulips. The place ran warm, so Mom had kept the window a smidge open. Jane, a former gymnast, raised one of her heels high and punctured the screen. She broke through it, then pushed the window open. I don't remember this, but heard Mom recount this scene repeatedly, often with an amused chuckle: "Then she just crawled up there to the window in her skimpy nurse outfit. She just jumped in, and anyone in the world could see her underwear. I don't know if you could call it underwear. Then she landed on the floor, and she went to unlock the door from the inside. Thank God for Jane Vaughan. I don't know what we would've done without her."

I don't recall walking to the apartment, or if Mom and Jane somehow carried me stretcher style. The next moment of lucidity came while I hunched over the couch, my gut wrenched. I wondered if death was near. I told God I'd never drink again. Mom offered me water. "Go away," I slurred at her. Jane came up with bread. "Matt, you have to eat something." I listened to Jane and ate.

That afternoon, Mom took care of me: soup, crackers, scrambled eggs. It amazes me now: she didn't chastise me. She didn't say, "What the hell were you thinking?" She didn't ask, quite rightfully, why I would put her in such a terrifying position. She didn't demand that I tell her why I had been compelled to drink myself to blackout. Her only mission the following day was to nurse me back to health. Perhaps she knew I was very skilled at making myself feel bad; her input was superfluous. The only way to help me was to care. Even as she must have wished to step in more and help, she resisted the urge, and allowed me to make my own mistakes. Perhaps she knew I'd just rebel against her practical, well-meaning gestures. I think of her reading *Saints for All Occasions* by Courtney J. Sullivan, which happened to be the last book she ever read:

She worried about the crowds he ran with, about his anger and his moods, about things he had done that could never be undone. She met her worries in the same old way. Whatever the hour, she would rise to her feet and climb the attic stairs to Patrick's bedroom, so that she might lay eyes on him. This was a bargain she struck, a ritual to guarantee safety. Nothing truly bad could happen if she was expecting it.

My struggles were my own. Like every parent, it must have pained her to watch all my hasty actions, my reactions to constant frustration, actions I'd soon enough regret. All she could do was watch and be there, ready to care for whatever was left of me after nights charging brick walls.

I attended the same university with Abby around this time, 2011. To my slight horror, Mom was set to finally finish her bachelors in 2012, my anticipated graduation, assuming my academic career was to take the standard four years. I say slight horror at this co-attendance because, though it offended my brutal sense of normality, it was pleasant to have the warmth of Mom around. I was glad she was studying. I was proud of her for removing the bands that had been placed around her intellect. Since she was a child in Potterville, since the military, since my father, all her surroundings were designed to retract her ability to grow.

As opposed to our life outside it, university was a stable, ordinary existence — a pleasant abnormality for us. I recall more quotidian joys than any dramatic event between the two of us. The most exciting thing we encountered at UAA was a bull moose wandering into the student union through the cafeteria's loading dock – before being spooked by the shriek of a few first-years – and turning 180 and running back to the woods.

We went to a few readings at UAA. We've always loved bookstores: fresh smells, quiet air, the infinite sense of possibility. She came along with me to a panel in the university bookstore. It featured three Alaskan novelists who each wrote a novella for this anthology. There were five people on stage and five people in the audience. I likely would have walked past the sparsely attended event – it was too uncomfortable to have people noticing me – and I loved Mom for joining me here, buttressing my meager courage.

The authors, who I automatically revered for being Authors, stepped up to a flimsy podium to read their work. I sat firmly upright, enraptured. Then it was suddenly time for questions.

With Mom at my side, I asked a question, something I was loathe to do in public. My question went to one writer in particular, who responded by saying I had good literary foresight, an assessment that made Mom turn to me and beam. Her too-apparent joy in any compliment toward me was, historically, cause for embarrassment; but at 21, I had (mostly) learned not to recoil from her pride.

The author asked me a question in return. I replied with a faltering voice and splotched neck. I tried to elevate the crown of my head closer to the ceiling in a "power pose." But all this accomplished was making me feel like a stretched chicken elongated against a cutting board. She asked me another question. I stumbled through my second answer, semi-successfully distracting everyone with a joke. Then at some point the conversation moved on, and I sank back down to the comfortable obscurity of my seat.

I wonder why this reading has figured so fondly in my life. I believe it was the first serious reading I attended. I went to lectures at Clark, but never readings or discussions of literature; scholars existed in my mind, thanks to the dense papers I often read from them, but living writers did not. And before Clark, the only bookstore in Anchorage to host authors of some repute would be Barnes & Noble, but those guests tended to write children's books, cookbooks or genre fiction that didn't interest me. Other visiting authors were confirmed literary superstars – David Sedaris, Louise Erdrich – who'd sell out before I could get a ticket. That panel at 21 with Mom was the first time I understood what living writers could look like and do. With these humble, homely figures who attracted audience members at a rate of 1:1, I sensed some possibility of writing and being published. Based on their warm camaraderie, the passion of the small-town publisher, it seemed worthwhile to write novellas, even if only one person ever cared to show up. That one person, for me, was Mom. That I felt the vibrancy of this vocation with Abby first will always mean so much.

Taco Bell, of all places, is another site of tenderness. One picture has become emblematic of our visits. Abby sits upright and perky, two thumbs way up; her smile is wild yet refined through the posture of posing, the faintest spectre of self-consciousness alights her smile. I admire her tight pink top, the white long sleeves. She's 48, exercises an hour a day, and all my female friends agree: Matt's Mom is hot.

Before her is our typical order: for $10.99 a dozen assorted tacos marketed as "The Family Pack." That the three of us share it – me going for the bean burritos, Grandma insisting that soft tacos aren't "real tacos," Mom happy with whatever's leftover – hits me with a pang. Oh, how Taco Bell's corporate office understood me more than myself. How well they knew what I took for granted, which pleasures moved in my gut that I couldn't articulate, or that I – in my constant dissatisfaction with present circumstances

— was too prideful to see. The three of us, "The Three Musketeers" as Abby called us, were family. More so than blood relations, we were a pack. Whatever difficulties assailed us, we climbed past them together.

I cannot tell you one explicit memory of the three of us together at Taco Bell. But I look at that picture of Mom and smile, feeling a shivery cry. The shiver comes from the absolute joy we shared, that, in her life, I could not fully appreciate. As a 17-year-old, I was thunderstruck by the closing of Sonnet 73: "This thou perceivest, which makes thy love more strong/ to love that well which thou must leave ere long." Even then, I was disappointed with myself for being unable to fully appreciate each moment of this passing life. I seemed incapable of grappling with what I loved, even as I knew the impending deadline meant that all this beauty would one day fall away; I had to look closely now — now was my chance to love and remember. But I, for whatever reason, was incapable: to make my love real through concrete action and to be a great friend, a great son who realized the love he was given. I perceived this all was coming to an end, but I could never sufficiently act.

The exact memories of us — touches, words exchanged, laughs — are unclear. They're just there, like all essential elements. They blend together into an invisible yet palpable form. These memories are omnipotent, if not militaristically specific. So many breakfasts and movies and park picnics I can't recall: between the three of us, then just Mom and me, then me and their memory. There are so many pointed moments I cannot exactly recall. Like a Seurat painting, moments of memory plant brilliant rings of color, but in approaching too close, they dissemble past figuration, overrun by negative space. Still, the feeling of being with them is blissfully overwhelming, even as others may only perceive outlines and sketches. I hear and see them in color warm and moving.

CHAPTER 13

Lawyers

When I was 21 in 2011, I worked as a low-paid admin assistant at a sketchy insurance company. Mom knew I was miserable. "God you hated that job," she'd laugh years later. On weeknights, I'd drive downtown to a gay bar, my left hand steering absently, my right with a stainless steel Kaladi Brothers filled to the brim with Coke and vanilla-flavored vodka. I was indiscriminate with who I fucked and who fucked me. Only if the other guy wanted protection did I mention there were condoms in my messenger bag. It amazes me that I never caught so much as a whiff of syphilis.

A year later, I moved to New York City. I never told Mom about working as a sex worker my first year in the city. (Would she have been familiar with the woke terminology, or would I have had to spell it out to her in more classical terms: her son was a gay prostitute.) She must have known I was doing something screwy in New York. From November 2012 to July 2013, I'd send her at least $800 cash every month. She never questioned where I got the money, or why I was sending hundred-dollar bills through the United States Postal Service. I told her I was just working as many jobs as I could find, which I suppose was true.

I had an unpaid internship with a tech startup. When a client asked for my presence in Boston or LA or Honolulu, I told her this startup was in a major growth phase, and I had to travel for work. The startup wanted me to grow with it as it scaled; the founders wanted to invest in me.

She was supportive and surprised, but not as overjoyed as when she learned that I was going to Clark, or when I got my first legitimate job at an American Apparel on Canal Street. Looking back, I sense that she didn't buy much of my act. But she was wise enough not to force a hard inquiry. At 22, I wasn't one for accountability. When people questioned me in ways I disliked, my response was to shut them out, or deduce some theory over them that defanged their judgment. I didn't see that this habit was in direct contradiction to my self-assessment as a free-thinking young man brave enough to stare down any Kafkian truth. My imagination was both irresponsibly boundless and irrationally constricted.

Perhaps if Mom had been healthy around this time, she would have pressed harder to know how I got my money. But in the fall of 2012, she was severely anemic, something she and her husband would hide from me until 2014. Iron was so sparse in her blood that some days she couldn't move her toes. Her sick days piled up. She lost her job as a rehab intake counselor: the rare, high-paying job that justified all those years in college.

I wonder if knowing about her pain as a 22-year-old would have knocked me from this orbit of self-absorption. While she couldn't get out of bed to work, I wept over the possibility that no one could ever love me as my last boyfriend did. As she was laid off for illness and struggled to find another good job, I routinely spent $80 on cocktails any given weekday. When a handsome jock picked me up from a bar, slept at my place, then didn't ask for my number in the morning, I pitied myself in bed for hours. I pitied myself for lacking the wealth to complete a prestigious degree, no family network to land me at a publishing house, no great intelligence to write an overnight bestseller.

As mom faced death, I flew to Palm Springs to spend a week with a corporate lawyer who previously had flown me to Hawaii and San Francisco. I earned $3,000 for each week-long trip. He was 42, good-looking, a power top — someone who I'd go on a date with in real life. He was happy to pay for all my meals, full-body massages at resorts, clothing sprees at Nordstrom's, and I was happy to imagine that none of this came with strings attached. I liked how intently he listened to Robert Schumann, that he wanted to write Grisham-esque potboilers, that he planned to whisk me away to Austria in November to hear a rarely-staged Brahms concerto. But by the second day of the Palm Springs trip, the onslaught of money apparently losing its allure, I started to recognize the lawyer's sheer narcissism. From our first phone conversation, it was clear he took pride in being "cool" and open-minded; his refrain was "I'm not like most lawyers." In the long drives with him around California, I slowly put together that he was a kind, lonely man whose range of topics was limited and circuitous: vacations he planned, cases he won, praise he had received from both friends and clients alike. By day three, I said I wasn't feeling well enough for sex. By day five, I snapped after burning my hand with coffee and complaining that the resort only had decaf. I sputtered that I wasn't attracted to him anymore.

"Really?" he asked.

"Yes. Sexually. I'm no longer sexually attracted to you."

My rather inelegant way of putting this ended our relationship. But he had already paid for another week, and instead of letting me stay in another hotel or with other friends, told me I would stay in his apartment in San Diego and sleep on the couch in his office.

The following days were palpably awkward. I did my best to leave the apartment before he woke up. I tried to feel no shame when he came home from work in his suit, saw me lazily reading in my shorts on one of his couches. I simpered. "Welcome home," I feebly said. He refused to look at me, and marched straight into his bedroom. The door slammed.

I asked to use one of his spare BMWs to visit a friend around Hollywood. To my surprise, he agreed. I had a drunken ball through several West Hollywood bars and stayed out long past the agreed time of midnight. Around 2am, he texted me in all caps: WHERE THE FUCK IS MY CAR. But before I could make up a lie, my phone died.

I was too drunk to drive back to San Diego. I walked to a few hotels with a friend, but everything was booked. An hour passed. We ate at Taco Bell. I downed a 24-ounce Gatorade. Nearing 4am, I said I was more than good to drive.

I wasn't. And the next two hours driving down the 405 were some of the most terrifying moments of my life. Every second I knew that I was playing with jail time. Mom had me take an intense driver's ed course with a gruff ex-military guy who'd shake his head at anyone going over the speed limit. Under a thick black mustache he'd huff, "It's a limit for a reason people!" He seemed to have found meaning in the constant laws of driving. "Remember, when someone steps into your car, they are placing their life into your hands. Take this responsibility seriously. Driving is a matter of life and death."

I rolled all the windows down, letting the thick wind claw my face. I hoped the hot sauce masked my tainted breath. The radio was set to a 90s station. I was the ideal driving student: straight back, a frequent observer of side-mirrors, running the motor at precisely 65 mph.

Right before 6am, I somehow made it safely to San Diego, the city (incidentally) of my birth. I didn't park my paramour's car in the garage, as requested, but in visitor parking. I tip-toed into his apartment, fortunately not waking his two pom-pom-sized dogs. I charged my phone and fell asleep soon as my body hit the couch.

I got up to pee around 9am. I ran into my employer in the kitchen. Coffee was brewing, and he was making eggs for himself. He hadn't replied to my string of mock-apology texts about my phone dying and traffic and having trouble navigating back to San Diego. When we locked eyes now, he stared at me with rage and disbelief.

What drove me to this destructive behavior? What were Mom's own close calls? What adventures of hers went off the rails?

I wonder if she ever had a year equivalent to my escapades as a sex worker in Manhattan. I met some of America's richest men, dudes who owned Fortune 1,000 companies, graduates (or provosts) of the country's finest schools, former Warhol superstars, men with several Tonys on their bookshelf. I found a certain freedom in sex work. It broke class boundaries, demarcations around sex and race; à la Whitman, it resisted internal and interpersonal divisions. By practicing sex work without shame, I was turning something scorned and unfairly criminalized into a cause for celebration. Sex work proved to me that in every chance encounter was a connection potentially profound; if only you would hunt for it, life (and all the strangers passing through) had meaning.

The more utilitarian reasons persisted: I needed money, I liked sex and was perpetually horny, I wanted material to write about, and my self-esteem was so weak that I needed a large, qualitative figure to justify my presence as something desirable. But the overriding reason why I found joy in sex work was the freedom to rewrite my past: all my life I had been told homosexuality was evil, and here I was now making a living out of it, exploring its every demonic crevice, building a life distinctly my own, a life that was exactly what the church feared, yet far more pleasurable than its wildest imaginings.

I wonder if Mom, as a very young woman, felt similar needs: to assert her freedom, her own path toward meaning. But instead of the infinitely porous world of sex work, she chose something that was infinitely rigid: the military. After a semester of attempting to endure nursing school in Lansing, she signed up with an on-campus recruiter to join the U.S. Air Force. This was around 1980. Like me with college, Abby was eager to leave the town she viewed as stifling.

I don't know where she was first stationed in the Air Force. But I know that she, like me at college, panicked the first couple of weeks there. She knew no one. She was far away from home. It was a frightening realization: that you, at the mighty age of 18, actually knew nothing about the larger world; that though you were deemed an adult, you couldn't fend for yourself.

Abby returned to Potterville after strategically flunking a test to get out of the Air Force. For another six months, she was an assistant manager at Little Caesars Pizza. She had fun with her childhood friends. She declined a manager role because she wanted to keep having fun and the pay bump didn't justify the added responsibilities. I've always loved this image of a 19-year-old rejecting a promotion because she'd rather focus on living: seeing movies with her friends, whispering about boys at sleepovers, or driving around in her friend's parent's leased convertible.

But before long, she was bored again and full of wanderlust. She wanted, like me, to explore the wider world. For exactly what, we couldn't tell you; but it was sure to be great. I think of *Moby Dick* here, Ishmael deciding to chase the "portentous and mysterious monster that roused all my curiosity: with other men, perhaps, such things would not have been inducements; but as for me, I am tormented with an everlasting itch for things remote."

She didn't join the Navy like her three older half-brothers. Perhaps joining the Marine Corps was an act of defiance for young Abby.

In a letter she wrote me the last month of her life, Mom said that the Marine Corps was the best and worst time of her life. The best lay in seeing new places, meeting people from walks of life she never thought to imagine. She met my father, which led to Lee Ann and me, "her babies," she called us well into our 20s. She told us over and over that we were the best decision of her life.

As sour as their relationship became, Mom and Dad did love each other once. My dad was a better man then — hopeful, open, funny, caring. He was wildly in love with Abby; she loved him too, but probably with the sort of ambivalence that I have inherited. Perhaps it was this ambivalence (where does it come from?) that led us to join extreme systems — me and sex work, she and the military — where our choices appeared to be ours alone, yet, by and large, were made for us.

She had her first child at 22. I can't imagine having a child so young. But maybe it worked for her, possibly providing the tether to reality she needed. But I can't help viewing this early grounding as confinement. She had to feel some resentment. In the months leading to her passing, she told me for the first time about her postpartum depression with Lee Ann.

She must have realized, too late in this case, all that having a baby implied. Aspects of her life were closed now, even as others opened. I don't doubt she had trouble accepting this tectonic shift. She was young — nearly 23! — and had more exploring to do. But her obligation was now to stay at home with the baby. I felt that I understood Abby's situation more when I read Adrienne Rich's essay, "Anger and Tenderness." Rich looks at her love and frustration with being a mother in the 1950s. "Even today, rereading old journals, remembering, I feel grief and anger; but their objects are no longer myself and my children. I feel grief at the waste of myself in those years, anger at the mutilation and manipulation of the relationship between mother and child, which is the great original source and experience of love."

In that final letter she wrote me, calling the Marines the best and worst of times, I think motherhood had something to do with these thoughts. Becoming a mother so early was, in some ways, rapturous; in others, a rupture with all her hopes for this life. She wrote that once their four years were up, troops chose one of three fates: to stay in the military; to move back home and settle down with "that sweetheart;" or take the "hot ticket" of marrying someone from the Corps and starting a new life. She and Dad decided on the "hot ticket" of marriage, even as neither of them knew entirely what to expect. And now at 54, she wrote that she was in a similarly unknown situation, but she had "faith" that experimental and fringe treatments would work.

Mom and Dad, when they were young, took pleasure in risk. I heard stories of Dad, then 19, jumping off the roof of his three-story fraternity house onto a couple of used mattresses. I look up Midwestern State University now, and see Wichita Falls' top attractions include a railroad and wrestling museum. Recent pictures of the university show bonfires and white people around a wood effigy, shouting, cupping their hands to echo their hollers. I can easily see Dad being the first to light one of these 20-foot-tall wood plank towers. In his second semester, he woke up on someone's lawn, stale vomit dried and crusty on his shirt. He joined the military the next day.

Abby and Dad found direction in the Marine Corps, but the roads they went down were not entirely satisfactory. Mom never expressed her discontent in being a housewife. But I felt her frustrations growing up, something that likely redoubled her frustration at failing to keep her disappointment from her children. In videos from 1992, I hear Dad narrating a family outing to a park. He points to Abby about 30 yards away, exercising her stress out on an AstroTurf lot. She looks fed up with him. He jokes about her typical dissatisfaction. It strikes me now, the essential dry humor of my family. When we couldn't laugh, we exploded, so jokes at each other's expense were common. Our laughs carried a slight malice that happier families lack.

Dad was fine being a police officer in LA, but he was never really happy. Growing up, he'd tell me he should've been a lawyer. He'd mention a string of fraternity brothers, or friends from the military. They all were in real estate now. Or sitting in their corner office of some manufacturing company. When he re-married at 38 to a lawyer and set up a real estate business, it was a case of wish fulfillment.

It saddens me: my parents' unfilled dreams. Mom dead. Me no longer speaking to Dad. My inability to understand their pain before it was too late. The arrogant optimism that we drive our fate.

CHAPTER 14

Princeton

In 2014, Mom accepted a research job through Princeton University. It sounds prestigious, and I enjoyed telling people my Mom was a research fellow at Princeton, but in truth, some post-docs in mathematics were just desperate for someone to collect data on how Native kids in remote Alaskan villages learned arithmetic.

I was living with my boyfriend Adam in Manhattan. Mom still lived in Anchorage, in a cozy house on the Northeast side we had shared together for three years. I hadn't seen her in six months. She never explicitly told me she missed me because it might make me feel bad, or under some obligation to fix her longing. In retrospect, it's obvious that she only took that paid training in Princeton, New Jersey (which we understood was somewhere near New York City) to be closer to me. I was in my mid-20s and didn't think much on how she missed me. All our daily calls ended with "I love you."

I had a miserable job as an administrative assistant at the Plastic Surgery ward of NYU Medical Center. My schedule only let me see her on Sunday. I'm amazed I didn't take more time off, or clear at least another day. Her training was only for a week. She had travelled 4,000 miles to be near me. Even if she were busy with classes most of the time, I could've traveled to Jersey for dinner more than once. But I didn't want to believe she needed me to do that, and she didn't explicitly ask; otherwise, I would have gone, potentially grumbling to myself at the inconvenience. I suppose that Abby gave me freedom and love, but ultimately, little direction.

We walked everywhere that Sunday in Princeton. The town was cute, all tidy and orchestrated to signal perfection. Mom was with a few other research assistants who had also agreed to a year-long assignment in the Alaskan wilderness for a free week-long trip to Jersey. They were White, voluble, and blonde. Like Mom, they were single mothers who wanted to do good by the world. I did my best to charm them, wanting to make Mom appear special. It worked. One hit on me and another suggested I join them for drinks. Mom shut them down. I was surprised how quick we were to leave them. Abby was one to entertain telemarketers for minutes and apologize before hanging up. She was jet-lagged, I reasoned.

The campus was undeniably beautiful. I kept trying to square the beauty of Princeton with the reality of its graduates, several of whom I knew to be fantastic assholes. In a crowded Italian restaurant, we sat close to two 19-year-olds talking about astrophysics. They didn't seem like assholes — courteous voices, creative insight. Nor was Princeton lacking in art. Its collection still amazes me. The institution was not all evil, even if it was the last Ivy to accept female graduate students and its most famous president, Woodrow Wilson, was an avowed racist. Princeton was snooty and repressive, but it also corralled people like Scott Fitzgerald, Sonia Sotomayor, Eugene O'Neill.

Mom didn't have much of an appetite. I forget if she drank any wine. Distantly, I was disappointed that my mother wasn't one to feast like the other parents in the restaurant, moving their forks and wine glasses around with such assurance. Now I wonder if she felt intimidated by the surroundings: the poised, privileged, gifted girls seated next to us. Or maybe it was my own insecurity that they were privy to each word of our conversation that couldn't match the particulars of theirs. Or perhaps it was the illness growing.

We walked everywhere and bought simple trinkets — popcorn, postcards, hot coco with marshmallows. We kept moving and didn't step into any of the shops. We were content to gawk from the outside, comment to one another, and move on with our stroll. We heard a football game start, and walked in the opposite direction.

I felt at once inferior to and disdainful of Princeton. Private schools, under my father's dictatorial eye, were for pansies. In California, I grew up praising public schools and mocking private universities. USC was for duds, Stanford was a disgrace because of the disorderly conduct of its marching band. At eight, Dad came home from work at the Los Angeles Sheriff's Department with a brochure from UCLA. "This is a good school," he told me. "It's for everyone." I still recall the texture of that glossy blue, matte paper. I didn't know exactly what college was, but I knew I'd be going there.

But to my father's grave disappointment, I attended Clark University, a private school whose motto was "Challenge Convention. Change Our World." He was determined not to spend a dime on a school that pushed a "liberal" curriculum focused on the so-called arts. He agreed to pay for books related to business and science only. He had made more money in real estate, and I hadn't expected this arbitrary line. My father had always told me that if I got good grades, college would be paid for. His parents couldn't pay for college, and he always felt cheated compared to his peers. The sting wasn't something he'd pass on to his son. But, ultimately, my father was a man of innovative values. His word was malleable, as suggested by his favorite dictums — "Do as I say, not as I do;" "It's not what you say, it's how you say it;" "If you know what I mean, why does it matter how I say it."

But Mom valued education. Mom loved that I was going to Clark. She loved the campus, the culture, the motto, and especially the Latin engraved on its walls: *Fiat Lux*. Let there be light.

In our quiet way, we were aspirational. She home-schooled me during fifth grade to allow more time for figure skating.

"Well Matthew," she asked me on our first day of fifth-grade homeschooling, worksheets spread around the dinner table. "What shall we call our school?"

We held our pencils at the ready. We were filling out demographic information about our school to be sent to the distant land of Maryland, specifically to a private school center that cost $800/semester (a figure I recall because of my father's repeated outrage). We considered what we both wanted from this experience. I wanted to be a professional figure skater. Mom wanted to help me get there. We settled on *Gold Medal Elementary*.

From middle school on, I sensed I'd be the first in my family to graduate from a four-year college, but I had no idea where I'd end up. I knew I had to get out of Alaska. The University of Alaska, Anchorage, referred to by my AP friends as *The University of Average Achievers*, was not an option. Everyone knew about Harvard and Yale, but the thousands of other possibilities were nameless to me.

The summer before college, I worked at Forever 21. A coworker asked where I was heading for school. "Oh," I said neutrally, as we waited in line for espresso. "Harvard." Her face lit up, eyes wider with attention than any of my previous comments earned. "Really??" She asked. "No," I said laughing. "Just kidding. I'm going to a small school in Massachusetts called Clark University."

"Oh," she said with flat disappointment.

But in Alaska, at least in my circles, no college name be-side Yale and Harvard carried gravitas. I first realized Princeton was a good school at 17, after watching Hillary Duff and Chad Michael Murray in "A Cinderella Story." I did not really understand what Cornell was until I was 22 and trying to live in the city. I've always felt a smidge of regret that I didn't even apply to a reach school, or prepare myself for some college whose utterance would trigger that surprised "Really??"

Mom likely felt a similar disappointment. She had an associates from College of the Canyons, a community college outside of LA, in math and science. She'd been to nursing school twice, but dropped out each time with a semester or a week left till graduation. Her rationale: she could not compassionately treat patients anymore, and she didn't wish to spend her professional days wiping butts.

"I try to love them all in some way," she told me. "I really do the best I can to be kind. But I just feel myself getting angry and frustrated. People don't deserve that energy when they're trying to heal."

She returned to college around my junior year. I delayed my official graduation date for years because of an outstanding math requirement (I had also come under the curious belief that a double major would get me far in life). Mom graduated before me, in 2012, at the age of 49. I have flattered myself in thinking that I was the first in my family to attend a national university, which is true, but it's inaccurate to say I was the first in my family to graduate from college. The first to graduate was Abby. She'd beat me to a master's degree, as well.

Mom was tired throughout that Sunday visit at Princeton, and all I could chalk it up to was jet lag. But she was 51 then, and what was diagnosed as stage IV colorectal cancer at 53 was likely growing. If she felt herself unusually ill, she may have attributed that to anemia, but she couldn't, as I couldn't, imagine her body with cancer.

Whatever pain she felt, she hid from me. As was the case for most of our life together. She never wanted me to feel the full weight of a harsh world. She shielded me as a child, then as a teen. At 27, when I became her primary caretaker, she shielded me from her thoughts. I had hints of the horror watching her stare at a white wall for hours, or at 100 pounds, fallen on the floor, delirious. "Ammonia" – an excess of which signals a failing liver – was a chemical I'd learn to fear. Abby never articulated her own frights. Her mission was to spread joy, not suffering. No matter what.

I imagine in locked arms we kept walking around Princeton, me oblivious to her suffering. We kept marveling at the impossibly tall oaks, the stone pavements stretching for miles, the courtyards well-curated, the churches solidly made from the finest brick. I remain astounded for all she did for me. When I became fully committed to pretension at 16, she went along with my new interests. I'd ask if she wanted to join me for yoga classes at The Alaska Club South. The classes began at 5:30 or 6am. She'd often say yes, even when fatigued in ways I couldn't imagine. Then I'd get annoyed with her yawns on the drive over there. She'd half-ass several poses, or stay in Down Dog too long. If I glared at her, she laughed it off and smiled. When Dad's income negated all my need-based aid for college, she took on loans and asked her father for money. She was so determined that I go to a good school that she took on extra shifts as a maid above the Arctic Circle, changing beds for oil workers on The North Slope. She didn't have to pay for food or rent up there, and the 14-hour shifts resulted in some serious overtime. Yet for all her efforts and my measly fast-food income, we were just below the national poverty line.

When I was nasty or depressed or drunk in my early 20s, she forgave me. When I was away in New York, rabid with my own life, she continued to text and send inspirational Bible verses, dog memes, and cut-out clippings from *The Anchorage Daily News*. Several of her emails signed off with, "Hope your day turns sunny."

CHAPTER 15

Mustangs on Clearance

2001 was a low point in our lives. Mom was looking for work. The car rental place had called the cops on us for keeping a green Neon Dodge three weeks passed its due. Some days we lived on Ritz crackers and Top Ramen. But in an act of divine grace, the church gave us a Mustang, free of charge. To call it beat up is to be kind: the Mustang's deep blue had been frayed by a million scratches into a metallic tawdry grey. It once had all of its original windows until some "bored punks," according to the pastor, threw a brick at its passenger window. It had, as Grandma called them, Devil Handlebars — chipped chrome skulls with red stickers in their gouged-out eyes à la *The Terminator*. Mom paid to replace the Devil Handlebars before she fixed the faulty headlight.

Desperate for any mode of transportation up and down the mountain, Mom and Victoria couldn't believe the good news. To Mom, the sudden gift of the Mustang signaled that her severance of a past life was the right move. The Mustang marked the beginnings of our adventures in Alaska; and years later – when I encouraged her to sell it – became a sign of my inevitable departure from her (Striking: I always imagined myself to be the one leaving).

Writing about the Mustang was my first foray into being a "writer" (odd — I hated that car so much growing up; who knew what good would come from it). I was staying on a friend's couch over winter break in New York in 2013. He was at work, so I had the quiet apartment to myself for days. After my last semester at UAA, I planned to move to San Francisco, Boston, or back to New York. In the quiet of that apartment, I suppose I started to think what this move would entail. Just what were my memories from Alaska? What had formed me, and who was this person I was about to leave? The answers felt wrapped up in the Mustang.

Soon as I realized what a memory-filled object the Mustang was, everything about our life together poured out. Mom and Victoria, the joys and frustrations — our lives had centered around that little car that got us everywhere. Scenes came to me without effort. Victoria – "a squat woman who wore Rudolph sweatshirts and leopard tights on Sunday mornings" – descending the church with tears in her eyes because the black church gave us a car; riding to work with Mom at 3:30am, from the top of Lazy Mountain on into Anchorage, with a passenger window gone and one headlight — "To avoid the ice wind coming at me at 65 mph, I crawled in the back. When I was too tired to crawl in the rear, I just reclined as far back as possible. Horizontally, the wind sliced past me. It was a neat view. Semi-trucks tended to ride our bumper; their floodlights illuminated the entire interior. I opened my eyes and saw particles swarming into the car. I watched space go by."

All the scenes compiled themselves together into what I'd later learn to call a "personal essay." I called the essay "Mustangs on Clearance." The title made small sense, but felt right. I was considering events 12 years gone; the logic mattered less than truth. "Life is not what one lived," Márquez writes in *Living to Tell the Tale*, "but what one remembers and how one remembers it in order to recount it."

That essay was the consequence of writing in journals since I was 11, coming to me far easier than the fiction I shared with boyfriends at 22. At the prompting of some friends, I applied to a highly competitive writing program in New York, and to my shock was accepted. I studied with authors I idolized. One said that each writer has only one, truly necessary memoir. I considered this to be bullshit. But looking at "Mustangs on Clearance" five years later, I wonder if he hit on a certain kind of truth. I suppose the essay was a condensed version of what I hope this memoir more elegantly conveys: the rich love we shared each to each: Grandma, me, Mom.

It's 2019 now, October 29th to be exact. I am 29 (So many nines, so many edges and borders approaching, life on the cusp of turning). My mother stopped breathing at 5pm in Anchorage, Alaska in 2017 on October 3rd. She was 54.

Abby watched Victoria, 87, pass on May 11, 2016. Five months later, cancer gripped her on a plane heading to Chicago; an ambulance was called to pick her up on the runway. Her diagnosis was 2–3 years. She died in 11 months.

Abby said she locked eyes right with Victoria before she left. Or locked eye. Poisons weren't leaving Victoria's body; her poor kidneys were defeated. I was aghast to see her on a video call a couple of days before she was gone — suddenly comatose. I panicked, and blamed Mom. I told her I wanted to see Victoria again; I wanted to say goodbye in person. "I'm sorry Matthew," she said, staying calm. In the face of my panic, she was always the bedrock. "It happened so suddenly. She was having good and bad days, but nothing like this. I'm sorry, Matthew." I did not think to more effectively comfort Mom, who was losing her mother, whose bond was just as strong as ours.

Out of one eye, Victoria looked at Mom with the compacted force of their entire history – a star reeling into itself – then closed. Eyes shut. She let go. Victoria released one last exhalation. Then, on this plane of reality, was gone. A star transmuted beyond human understanding.

Mom, the perpetual optimist: "You could feel her leave us," she told me over the phone, her voice affecting grace, me walking up Second Avenue after the gym, thankful that my bright orange sunglasses hid the tears. "In a way, it was actually peaceful." After her Mom stopped breathing, she and her two half-siblings went for a coffee.

"How are you all doing today?" The barista asked brightly.

"We're doing fine, thank you," Mom said.

"Actually," said her half-sister, Rhoda, who has always been a bit more hard-nosed and realistic. "Our mother just passed."

The barista issued effusive apologies to these three people, aged 50 to 70, who for the past month had become cafe regulars. She said that each of them could have an extra shot on the house. Mom said this as if the barista was extending a great kindness; I wondered then and continue to question now — three free shots? — that was the best you could do?

On the M train home today, I came across some poems of grief that Mom would admire. Two lines from Robert Hayden kept returning, perfect distillations possible only at the death of a parent:

> *What did I know, what did I know*
> *of love's austere and lonely offices?*

Mom's own death was harrowing, the decline quick, the death itself long, often (how I wish it was otherwise) ungentle. She was not ready to die at 54. She had just completed a master's program in social psychology; both of her children were heading toward marriage; she and Jeremy had rekindled their love. Her final day was, perhaps, a wrestling labyrinth between accepting death and absolute resistance to passing. She likely was terrified; she likely was relieved. I can only imagine the words she wanted to speak.

She was immobile. But her eyes told me everything. The turning chapters of her life – the horror, the immense gratitude, the indignation, the giddy hope, the joy; I could feel her writhe and rage with a yelling mouth; I felt her smile, at times immensely content. She lay in a makeshift bed from hospice. The living room was one we had occupied for less than a year. In her line of vision, I tried to assemble everything comforting: a wood carving of a horse galloping, stuffed animals we had collected over the years, pictures of Grandma, of me and Lee Ann, soft Christian music in the background, lit candles, the smell of vanilla. I bent over her sickbed, which I knew was her deathbed. I forced the biggest smile on my face, the face that was her own. "When you want to go, you can," I told her. I was smiling as tears dropped out of my eyes onto the comforter. Saltwater blurred my vision. "We will take care of each other," I told her. "You will always be with us."

Her last breath was to "Amazing Grace." The Darlene Zschech version, the singer who had accompanied us on that terrifying trip up the mountain.

In this life, I will never know for certain if she accepted death, or if it came for her. Grandma, by Mom's reckoning, let go with one long breath. But with Abby, breath was taken from her. It could be entirely physiological, as the hospice chaplain told me. "Air hunger," was what she called the entire body gasping. Perhaps Mom was trying to let go. Dying, I've been told, can be hard work; the body, like some obstinate software program, incapable of shutting down. I can scarcely imagine anything more agonizing than this immobile death: to know and feel your body shutting down, to be paralyzed and breathing, to simply wait for death to take, to not know in the last moments when it will come and if it's there.

I wrote "Mustangs on Clearance" when Mom and Grandma were alive. Perhaps those thoughts welled up in New York because I sensed, by graduating (finally) in May 2014, I wouldn't return to Alaska. They sensed it too. I have a photo that Mom took. It shows Grandma, her usual short self, hugging me tightly at the doorstep of 1513 Atkinson, Mom's two-bedroom apartment in East Anchorage. I wrap my arms around her, and lean in closer. Our heads tilt in toward each other. We both know what's happening; and Mom, behind the lens, had to know, too.

On my friend's couch in New York, I had to be thinking about the great times the three of us had, the complicated relationship I had with Mom, the bond I scorned at times, yet ultimately valued above all else. In writing that essay, I assumed that I would be leaving her. I was summoning the memories to justify my departure; life had been challenging in Alaska, and growing up there had put me behind socially, intellectually, economically. I recalled the specific dangers: the rickety Mustang, the knife-marked apartment, Grandma's mice-infested house. But I also wanted to bottle up the love in talismans to accompany me wherever I landed: her joy when I got into college, her constant love of those creative aspects of my personality that others called queer, how we huddled under blankets in the "Blue House" on the outskirts of Wasilla in -25 F, hot cocoa shivering in our hands. Now, I sit in wonder at the amazingly self-serving impulses that made that essay: how secure I was in the belief that she would never leave me.

The title, "Mustangs on Clearance," remains a puzzle to me. Its logic borders the nonsensical. There was only one Mustang, and it wasn't on clearance — it was free. But following the logical truth – "Mustang for free" – would bring none of the emotion imbuing our days. "On clearance" pointed to the demarcations surrounding our desires — that we were limited in what we could afford and understand. "Mustangs on Clearance," then, was our mental, political, and economic situation: we grabbed what we could afford, resulting in a collection of memories that are both magnificent and pathetic, devastating and affirming.

This memoir began on September 12th, 2019, in the widening days since her death on October 3rd, 2017. "One Headlight" refers to the Mustang. To our life together: scrappy, loving, dangerous, at times illegal. That one light has become a dinky paean to our relationship. I consider all the trips we took, the plans we had, the trials and triumphs that made us. I stand in awe of her ability to raise me and love me no matter what. Without much support, the two of us drove to our shared and respective dreams. Our paths diverged, but overwhelming is my incontestable sense that we made it. With one headlight, we made it.

Part Two

From the death of my mother, the world began to dissolve around me, beautiful, iridescent, but passing away substanceless. Till I almost dissolved away myself, and was very ill, when I was twenty-six. Then slowly the world came back: or I myself returned: but to another world.

—D.H. Lawrence, *Letters*

CHAPTER 16

Lit the World

The Mustang had been gone for years. Literally sold for spare parts. Mom grieved its passing while I celebrated the sloughing of poverty. We had gotten by on a white Jeep Cherokee since 2007, but for 2011 to be a functional year, we needed a new vehicle and couldn't rely on the erratic public bus system charmingly called The People Mover.

Mom had resisted a new car for months. There was nothing left to pay on the Jeep, and we finally owed no one. But, I maintained, the damn thing needed repairs so often the Jeep was like having a new car with none of the benefits. Once a mechanic told Mom that a radiator repair would put us back $850, her stubborn defense of the jeep finally dropped.

We test drove new cars in December. Test driving in the middle of winter may seem like a bad idea, but we figured if a car could handle itself in the worst of times, the summer would be a breeze. The first car was a beige oblong thing with front-wheel drive. It was like the Mustang in that regard, but lacked the character to stay grounded during tight turns in the snow. I took one turn fast, the car's tail nearly hit a semi-truck as the sales guy yelped.

We got lucky with the second car: hatchback sedan, sinuous exterior with blue metallic paint that glinted from the snow. The Toyota Matrix was all-wheel drive. While I always pictured Toyotas in drier lands like California, the hatchback surprised me with how well it gripped snowbanked roads. We felt a rare security in the Matrix, habituated as we were to a missing window and one working headlight.

I don't recall how Mom settled on the name "Matey." She was excited for a brand new car, a treat we hadn't experienced in over 15 years. To capture her giddiness, she needed a name. She wanted to show gratitude and pride that our mutual effort had resulted in something worthwhile. She had learned from the Mustang to appreciate precious objects before they vanished.

The nickname, "Matey," annoyed me. Perhaps I withstood it because I was finally learning how not to be an asshole, and to accept Mom's harmless peculiarities. I, too, was excited for the new step in our life. I needed the name, but I was too pretentious and cowardly to accept the sentimentality. At times, I told her the nickname was dumb, but within a year, I had to consciously stop myself from thinking of the Matrix as "Matey."

We had quite a few laughs in Matey — trips to the Matanuska Valley, moving Grandma about Wasilla, Taco Bell drive-thrus, picnics at Westchester Lagoon. But, to my slight disappointment, what I really recall about Matey is all the fucking I did in its backseat. I wonder what it says about me that my memories of swapping head with a Mormon guy in 2011 are as vivid as one of my last drives with Mom. That I recall holding hands in Matey with the first man I really loved, but only once holding Mom's hand after a chemo appointment. I'm not sure what to make of this situation — that I treated "my" car as a mobile sex dungeon. Perhaps I shouldn't feel so bad. If the actions of others point to an appropriate morality, then I am not the only college student who, living with his parents, used his car for sexual encounters with, say, a Cinnabon employee, a professional oboist, and a hydroponic gardener.

But what puzzles me, is that even as my mother lay dying in a rented apartment, I used the car – our Matey – for sex. I spent several evenings in a dark park with a guy named Weston having toe-curling sex. Before one of Mom's appointments, I rushed to a stranger I found on Scruff. I had him fuck me against a wall in his midtown apartment.

The affair was maybe three minutes. He came in me, then said his boyfriend would be home soon and I should leave now. I was buttoning up my shirt when I locked eyes with his boyfriend half-way down the stairs.

The sexcapades were partially to relieve the physical burden of becoming Mom's primary caretaker at 26. The other part was distraction. Sex is the opposite of death, and spending days with her where she could hardly move her head, or could do nothing but blankly contemplate the enormity of a white, stucco wall — I needed a distraction from the horror. As Georges Bataille puts it, "Eroticism is assenting to life even in death."

As with so much of life, literature explained things to me. Once paramedics came to take her to the hospital, once her crippled form seemed certain to never resurrect, I went into vigil. I didn't know what was needed of me until I turned to an essay by Kathryn Harrison, "Keeping Vigil." It documented her reaction to the death of her father-in-law, a kind man who had become a surrogate father against her abusive birth father. My mother had less than a year to live since her diagnosis, and during that time, I was always busy trying to do something more: move her to more comfortable surroundings, keep in touch with her friends, send flowers, take care of bills. But after I found her on the floor one day, I recalled that essay: the necessary patience, the foreignly intimate stage of death, preparing the distance from someone cherished, an acceptance of helplessness. What our situation required now of me was vigil: to simply watch, to no longer act.

Death required waiting. Eventually, it required sitting around doing nothing as your beautiful adventure writhed in realities none of us can know until we've been. Keeping vigil requires a rabid peace, a thrashing apathy where you must loosen the frenzied hand over the reins you believed had the power to hold you two together. That this would be demanded of me, I couldn't know. That I had an essay to adumbrate this necessary state did, somehow, ease the pain of entering it.

Sharon Olds, too, helped explain my gross pains and sex drive. I thought of her poetry around craving sex on the day of her father's funeral. In the months and weeks leading up to Abby's death, I was horny. Perhaps Mom would have been a bit proud at the vivacity of my simple urge. I imagine her laughing, "Hey, whatever makes you feel alive, I say go out and live!" And live I did — telling her I was picking up orange juice from the grocery store when I planned to ride on the massive, beautiful, and pulsating hard dick of an older fuckbuddy. I left her for quick blowjobs in the house of some stoned guy I didn't know. I left her to watch Netflix by herself for hours so that I could get fucked in the parking lot of the Buckaroo Club on Spenard. What is it about one's 20s that makes it so easy to disregard those who love you more than anything? Or is the truth so simple that I am hardly a good person?

About 11 months after Abby's death, I rushed to Alaska. Word had it that one of Victoria's former friends, Barry, was unhinged. After three years in prison for aggravated assault, he had drunkenly mentioned around town that he was going to burn down Victoria's home. Years ago, she had let him live there for free, but now all the doors were locked by my stepfather, Jeremy, who checked in on the mountain every other month. Barry wanted in. And if he couldn't have it, why should he let it continue to stand?

When my stepfather told me this, I booked a flight from NYC. I landed two days later. I planned to stay a few days up there, searching for the objects I couldn't have burnt. Then I vowed to never drive up Lazy Mountain again.

With the help of a good friend and Jeremy, I was mostly successful. I grabbed Grandma's photos, some of the mono-chromatic jackets and glitz purses. The Lazy Mountain house was a shell of its former glory. Victoria hadn't lived up there for years. When Barry was in residence, he had brought a few cats up with him. They had grown and multiplied to over two dozen in short order. True to character, Barry never cleaned up after them, so they pissed and shat through-out the house, ruining many of Victoria's books and letters.

After Abby passed, Jeremy and his father moved to the mountain. Either they, or Barry, had small patience for Victoria's collections of dolls and barbies, and threw them all out. Gone, too, were the 200-plus Bibles Victoria had col-lected in her 87 years. Jeremy and his father fancied them-selves as fixer-uppers. They ripped out walls and windows and porches. They each left Alaska before they could replace everything. Gone were the brightly painted yellow and blue walls of the living room, the deep orange surrounding the kitchen.

I rented an SUV in Palmer to voyage up to Lazy Mountain. I'd grab everything memorable, I told myself, as I wouldn't ever be back. This would absolutely be my last time up the mountain.

But even in claiming to distance myself, I found myself attracted to it, wanting to fix it somehow. More than two years later, I still vacillate between selling and keeping the land. But going up to the mountain then, I was sure I had to say goodbye. Seeing its complete devastation, the smell of mold layered over a thick whiff of excrement, I had to ac-cept that the house I learned to love no longer existed. But acting on that knowledge – distancing myself entirely from this past – was a challenge I couldn't yet meet.

In that hurried trip, I stayed with a close friend who had seen my Mom near the end, made food for us, always wanted to do more. My first day there, she lent me her pick-up truck to visit Abby's grave on the northeast outskirts of Anchorage. I tried to enact our rituals: a stop at Great Harvest Bread Company for their famous breakfast panini; a mocha at the Kaladi Brothers on Tudor, the one far east with the best views of the mountains. I asked for an extra cup at Kaladi Brothers; they smiled, and didn't ask what for. The texture and curve of that cup were deeply familiar to us. The red-white schemes with the prancing goat logo that endeared us further to Kaladi. On one of these cups, I wrote a message in blue ink to Abby. I told her how grateful I was for her; I listed all the people who thought of her continually.

Good news came suddenly in the parking lot of Great Harvest, a job offer from a financial firm in Manhattan. The past two years of freelancing had unmoored me. The job insecurity, the constant negotiations of payment, the disrespect — it all frustrated me and nullified any ambition to wake up early and push myself. Mom tried to view this situation optimistically: I was writing summaries of literary classics, forewords for a well-known imprint, arts articles for one newspaper, all while manifesting that "follow your heart but keep your head" dictate by writing marketing material for a software company. I made my own schedule and chose my bosses. But she didn't seem to get how precarious my professional life was. My health insurance was federally subsidized and hinged on the election cycle. I had no savings; my random assortment of gigs was building no discernable career trajectory. I wanted a gratifying, stable job, and I was indignant that no one helped me reach that state, that I (bolstered by Mom's free spirit) thought it was normal to quit jobs during a lunch break, stay at others for seven weeks, and bounce from one industry that had nothing to do with the next.

I vented to Mom about my professional disappointments. She replied by telling me she thought I had a pretty good job. Her tone struck me as terribly naive. I exploded: "Freelancing is an awful life. I wouldn't wish it on my worst enemy."

I laugh at my melodrama now, but her face grew crestfallen when I told her that. I was confronting her with a fact (just one of many) that rattled our existence: that all our dreams would not come true, that the world was staid and grey and would not change no matter how long we insisted on color. I burn with shame at how I spoke to her. That I was intensely unsatisfied with my job implied that all her sacrifices were for naught: staying in versus going out with friends, paying for my college by working on the North Slope, the custody battle for me against Dad. All her efforts were to give me the best life. And she did, in the grand scheme of things — I do believe I would have done something irreversible if I had remained under my father's roof. For all the trials we faced, I'd take her love over his material comfort any given second. But in that outburst, my frustration aimed to hurt her. And I did. I'll always remember that look of gentle shock – hopes dashed – and I will never forgive myself.

Perhaps it was this guilt and regret that charged my reaction to that job offer in the parking lot of Great Harvest. It seemed too fortuitous that on the way to visit Abby's grave for the first time, I happened to receive the offer I had been hoping to gain for years. Later, I'd joke that she had called in some heavenly favors.

I pounded on the rustic steering wheel of my friend's pickup truck (having briskly sold Matey after the funeral, only realizing what I had done once the keys left my hand). I found myself repeating, "Mom, we did it." I smiled through tears.

I pulled up to the military gate. I flashed my permanent visitor's pass.

"We did it Mom," I said laughing, lo-fi manic, as I drove down the sternly cut lawns, the mile-long roads with nothing in between; on the way to the funeral, the occasional incoming car slowed and edged to the side of the road. Something about that simple act of generosity, acknowledgment, and respect will always stay with me.

I placed a hand on her tombstone. "Her smile lit the world," the inscription read. I placed the empty Kaladi cup at the base, along with multi-colored roses I'd picked up from Fred Meyer.

I talked to her. I breathed in the cool air, September's sunshine. I kept talking. I told her how much I loved her, how sorry I was. I did not ask for forgiveness. I do not feel that I deserve forgiveness.

Eventually, I sat cross-legged. I fiddled with the grass above her. I told her about the new job, and I felt her delight, hugs, excitement. I told her that Adam had received a promotion and that we were living on 73rd Street now, that all my friends and her friends were well, that we thought of her all the time. I could see her smile. Her hands coming together in a clasp of joy.

CHAPTER 17

Alive

Our relationship had rarely been so strained as it was the summer of 2016. Grandma had died. Mom didn't know how to deal with the loss other than carrying on with unflagging optimism. She found comfort in the Pentecostal reorientation of death as not the end but the beginning, that rebranding of *RIP* as *Rest in Power*.

I also was no good at responding to death. Like Mom, I tried to see things positively, but my lens leaned humanist rather than spiritual. I accepted death, and tried to remind myself of the once living joy: we had stories together; at 87, she had lived! She had been loved, had three children – including Mom – to help her pass. Mom accepted death too, but what solace she could find came in the belief that they would meet again in a world beyond this one. No doubt, her faith in heaven was shaken, just as mine in the power of stories to hold a person's being was shaken, but neither of us lost faith that in some sense Victoria's life continued.

I didn't understand the magnitude of Mom's loss. Mom, who never wanted to inconvenience anyone, did not show the cracks in her soul, at least nothing legible to my gauzy perception. Yes, we cried on the phone. We reminisced. But I did not realize she needed me to comfort her (it's such an obvious need, looking back). Only when she passed and I flipped through her journals did I gain an ineluctable clue: "Matthew is sad, but he doesn't realize I lost my mother."

In the summer following Victoria's death in San Diego, Abby traveled randomly across the US. She did not wish to return to Alaska straight away, in part, I think, because the reason she had moved up there years ago – Grandma – was gone. Abby had stayed for several weeks in San Diego, working as a telemarketer after Victoria passed. She lived with distant relatives in Texas, Florida, Michigan. Then one day, she called me at work to say she had landed at JFK. Without any warning, I told Adam that the woman he fondly called Ms. Abby would be staying with us. It was only a week, but in our one-bedroom, railroad-style apartment, where Adam and I had to walk through her sleeping on the couch to grab some water or use the bathroom, the inconvenience was undeniable. If she were one to ask for favors, we would have let her stay for a month, but she was determined to quickly "get out of your hair before too long."

Mom had several interviews for social worker jobs. She applied everywhere: upstate New York, the suburbs of Trenton, western Connecticut. A rural outpatient network in New Hampshire hired her. They knew it was rare to find a personable, caring, mostly qualified candidate who was willing to drive about 4 to 6 hours a day to meet patients living far from any main road. But Mom loved driving. As a girl, even as a teen, she thought the coolest job in the world would be driving a giant truck — for that kind of horsepower, even collecting trash would be worth it. In the power of an 18-wheeler, you were free to explore America's highways. You could feel the wind run through your hair while blasting your favorite cassettes. You were independent. Your home followed you: a place to sleep, food to eat, a paycheck to spend on personal trinkets.

She must have found comfort in these long drives across New Hampshire and Vermont. She could think about Victoria. Their close relationship. She could talk to her friends for hours; she could talk to Victoria as if she were just in reach, buckled up in the passenger seat.

For a few months, Abby lived in northern New Hampshire, zig-zagging across the state from Monday to Friday.

I was happy that she had left Alaska. No one was quite sure what was up there for her: jobs were harder to come by, a higher cost of living, and her husband Jeremy seemed to be exiting the picture. While I didn't want to live on the same block, I wanted to be closer to Mom. So I sent her listings to cheaper places in New Jersey, along Metro-North. Concord and various towns around northern New Hampshire weren't ideal, being a six-hour drive away, but it was better than Alaska. And if that's where she chose to settle, so be it. I was happy so long as she stopped roaming around the States.

For the next couple of months, I thought Abby was making a stable life for herself in the Live Free or Die state. I was proud of her. I knew Victoria would be, too. I gave her thousands of dollars. I revised her cover letters and reformatted her clunky resume to help snatch a few interviews. But one day, after my job as a tutor in Harlem let out, she called my cell. She caught me in a frazzled mood, huffing toward the 6 train. It was loud wherever she was. I asked her how work was going.

"Oh. You know."

I asked where she was. More silence. The noise coming from both of our phones were similar. I asked again, with an impatient menace to my voice.

"Okay," she prefaced, "Don't be mad, but I believe I'm in Midtown?"

She had quit her job. She couldn't focus; the drives were too long; New Hampshire, simply put, bored her.

"But you signed up for that," I told her. "They were counting on you, no?"

Thus began an ugly summer of Mom grieving in ways I could not see or, as a selfish man in his 20s living in Manhattan, did not want to see. I got in fights with her (fights that made me feel worse because she never fought back). My one-sided debates revolved around her lack of planning, her sheepish requests for money, her sporadic, expensive purchases of a new dress or a new phone, that she was draining her family's resources when she had more support back in Alaska. I saw a series of erratic actions that belonged to a crazy woman. I did not understand that these were the lesions of grief. But I was too cowardly to help her with her pain. I was too selfish to see I was the only one, knowing Grandma so well, who could help her work through the loss. I lacked the fortitude and willpower to suffer with her. That I did not even fly to San Diego for the funeral for Grandma, citing finals for graduate school, may be the oculus to my pantheon of regrets and shame.

When she was too embarrassed to stay with me and Adam in our cramped quarters, she left for what she said was a motel. Later, I'd find out it was a homeless shelter. She'd take any job she could, including one for Postmates, becoming an expendable delivery person in one of the busiest cities in the world. After she passed, my heart sank to read some of the texts on her phone, people writing to her in all caps WHERE THE HELL ARE YOU. What resonance these messages took on a dead woman's phone.

She was hapless in New York, which can be expected when you move here as a 22-year-old, as I did. The city could forgive my cringe-worthy behavior, but not my mother's, a woman of 53. She applied to bakery jobs on the Upper East Side where everyone on staff was under 24. She applied to customer service jobs at software companies that required introductory videos to be uploaded onto their hyper-optimized platform; her videos came out with bad angles, poor lighting, a voice that underscored her discomfort.

I asked her to stay with me after I found out about the homeless shelter. She had already lost 20 pounds. She stayed with us another week. Then she was gone again – "I don't want to impose on you guys." She went to a women's shelter run by Veterans Affairs. It was at the end of the subway line in East New York. She got her own van-sized room; the other bed was never occupied. There were no decorations: white walls, beige carpets. It was a shelter, but not nearly as bad as where she had stayed in the East Village. She promised me it was more like a hostel.

Abby continued to try to make New York work. I grew frustrated with her that she just moved here without any respect for the competition, the city's summer heat, its meanness. I warned her about all of this. But she didn't seem to care, or considered these obstacles minor. Perhaps it was the grief thinking. Maybe she just wanted to be closer to me. She had this sad habit of imitating whatever I tried: ordering whatever I ordered, reading whatever I was reading, going to college because that's where my focus was, moving to New York because that was all I talked about.

Now that she's gone, it's easy to forget the pain her erratic behavior caused. On my finances and mental state. When it was clear she was impacting Adam and his family, I decided to draw a permanent line between us. Until she started acting sane and moved back to Alaska, I wasn't going to speak with her. I was creating a life and here she was, as was so typical from adolescence on, intruding. My rage darkened. At 17, after she had asked me for rent money for the new studio on Spenard; that's when I asked for the first time whether she was a bad mother. Now, seeing how she dragged me and those I loved along, I considered her other missteps: driving me through a snowstorm with one headlight, getting married to a man 20 years young and telling me four hours before, giving me essentially no supervision as a teenager, preparing me in no way for the real world. She meant well, but her actions were more impactful.

I thought being mean to her might make her return to Alaska. I was certain she needed to be with Jeremy. I told her I'd give her no more money, except for a ticket back to her home. I limited conversation to once a week. I gave her hundreds of dollars for food. When she requested more, I learned that most of the money had gone to a new phone and ostentatious clothing for an interview. All these supports and hopes I placed in her were routinely thwarted. It felt that this pain was unnecessary and caused only by her self-ishness.

Eventually, I told her I couldn't see her like this. It was the height of summer. She thought I was overreacting.

"But if that's how you feel, could you bring me a few tote bags with my things in them. They should be in your closet?" I agreed to see her one last time.

My blood boiled. She stood on 39th and Madison, holding a couple plastic bags. Abby looked homeless. I felt a surge of pity, also a terrible pain that if I continued to associate with her, she would drag me under. All the support I gave her seemed squandered. None of my friends experienced this situation of bleeding money to a parent; even Adam admitted it was stressful, unusual — that a limit had to be reached. She wore a purple spaghetti tank top. I dropped her belongings near her feet on the sidewalk. She moved in for a hug, but I brushed her off. Her hair was matted. Her body odor was sour.

"You are doing this to yourself, okay?" I said in an angry flash. "That's all I have to say to you."

I turned away. I hailed a taxi heading uptown. Distantly I heard her: "Wait Matthew, can we talk about this?"

But I didn't slow down getting into the cab. All our relationship, as I felt then, was talk. She had taught me that actions weren't everything, that God could see through your heart and know you're good. But now I was certain that good intentions, no matter how purely believed, meant shit. Acts mattered, and until she realized that, I was done with her.

I got in the cab and looked straight ahead. I was committed to not looking back, but the cab caught a light. Its motor hummed.

I looked back. Mom was still standing where I left her, looking blankly at the space where I had stood. She looked defeated. She sighed. Reached down like an old lady to pick up her bags from the ground. She heaved them on her thinning shoulders. She started walking slowly to wherever she was going.

I turned around to face north on Park Avenue. My jaw was clenched. Tears streamed down my cheeks. But as the cab went uptown and Mom headed south, I did not ask the driver to turn around. I did not try to save, or even help, my mother.

By the end of summer, New York had run its course, and Abby was ready for Alaska without her mother. But first, she insisted on collecting her suitcase from a mid-50s man who rented out a room to her in his house for $450 a month. From how Mom described him, I sensed that his regard toward her was not wholly innocent. Within seconds of meeting him, I saw this hunch was right. For some reason, this produced more irritation with Mom than disgust for the man; he was awful, no debate was needed (perhaps a sliver of me even thought that it was normal for a man to act out his ballooning lust). What chafed me was Mom's assent to this: to stay in some dude's house who likely fantasized about her every night. Why, I wondered, would she allow herself to live under the thumb of this guy. Looking back at my 26-year-old thoughts, I stand amazed by how rarely a man's empathy for women manifests itself as sympathy.

Mom insisted on driving up to this man's house then back to New York the same day as my one day off from teaching and working at a museum. Twelve hours of driving in and out of the city. None of the items up there were essential. It was all old clothes and flyers she had picked up from her travels around America. Neither the suitcase nor anything within it were worth the cost of the rented car and gallons of gasoline to get up there and back in the same day. The man even volunteered to ship it all to Alaska for free. Our trip, in my view, was pointless.

But Mom, for reasons I deemed agonizing and irrational, wanted all of her things before her return flight home. I finally agreed to this sudden, random road trip, thinking this would be her final, crazy request, then she'd be free to (as she had always wanted) to get out of our hair.

We picked up a red compact car from a Hertz on 76th Street. I was giddy with coffee, excited to start the day at 7am, happy to be with a stabilizing Mom. Mom wanted to be the driver. Ostensibly, our buddy dynamic had resumed. But then she'd make an obvious comment as we pushed through the Bronx, or asked me a dim question for the third time. I was quick to snap at her for taking the wrong road, even as I knew no better.

In my irritability, we didn't dwell on Grandma. I was too annoyed with her for asking me to rent a car for reclaiming some old clothes and free flyers. I thoughtlessly rejoined Mom's remarks on the blooming beauty of Connecticut, Massachusetts, Vermont. Along with the temporary insurance for two drivers, this stupid endeavor would cost far more than whatever was in that suitcase. This was a pointless journey. I smoldered silently.

My ego hampered me from realizing that was the point. Each mile was the chance to honor our relationship, to remember Grandma, the "crazy" woman who made everything possible. The closest we got to a real mourning was at a Panera Bread Company near Bryant Park. We were seated across from each other, enjoying soup and paninis, trading stories of Victoria. One of us choked up; the other followed. Soon we were holding hands across the table, bawling. "We sure did have some good times," Abby said between tears.

I slept during my respites from driving; Mom took a photo of my head tilted away from her. It shows my lips open, bulky orange sunglasses over my closed eyes, a blank and total sleep. I engaged in the sort of behavior I'd criticize my sister for at Mom's deathbed: playing music I wanted to hear, rather than something she loved. But fortunately, Mom and I shared tastes in music. When I played "I Giorni" by Ludovico Einaudi, she cried at the soft piano steps, the orchestra nearing apotheosis. I played Sia's acoustic album. Mom, to my delight, snapped her head my way when Sia belted "Alive," the towering octaves she'd hit in "Chandelier," the sliding sharps. We had always loved the sound of the human voice, especially one like a woman's, which belonged to a body thought not to be strong: Whitney Houston, of course. But also Celine Dion, Faith Hill, Jewel, Aretha Franklin, Adele.

Mom got sick just a month after this drive, having vomited on a plane from Anchorage to Chicago on the way to visit her father. Once the diagnosis seemed clear and the emergency operation complete, I flew to Chicago from New York, for the first time realizing my mother's fragility. I saw her in a green hospital gown and cap. I danced on occasion to make her happy: the Macarena, the Chicken Dance. I played Sia's "Alive," the acoustic version we had been held by just a month prior. She weakly danced with me. She teared up and smiled at the thunderous chorus:

I'm alive
I'm alive

I'm alive.

Only now am I putting together the connection that she first heard that song on the way to Concord, New Hampshire. Just as I could only now realize, in an earth-shattering sense, the cicatrix of her absence; just as I sense it will be too late before I know the weight of death as she did: her body steadily slipping from the heavenly declaration:

I'm alive
　　I'm alive
　　　　I'm alive.

CHAPTER 18
Opta Ardua

I've mentioned the drive to bury Abby was remarkable. The Air Force women and men didn't hesitate to move their cars to the side. They took the time to acknowledge a fallen peer. I can't say comrade. It seems too jingoistic to me (perhaps my inability to let in-groups operate as in-groups explains why I belong to few, if truly any). Regardless. How the military community moved to honor the body of my mother shook my core.

My family had never been one for ritual. Or perhaps, the conservative-leaning, militaristic-focused rituals they loved weren't ones I could easily join. But my place after the death of Abby was indisputable.

I sat at the center of several rows of white benches. My sister and her fiancé arrived shortly after. She sat several rows behind me. We were not speaking, and for the foreseeable future (if not for all of the future) I was content with that.

October 10th was icy. The sun was out, granting the evergreens a glossmeric sheen. The dozen or so cars coming from the funeral parked in single-file a good distance from the rotunda where the coffin was to be laid. We watched helplessly and patiently in the chill as the shoulders of four Air Force men brought the blue coffin (a color she would have liked, now that I think of it, similar in hue to Matey and the Mustang). They placed it – what remained of Abby – on a stand. At some point, they draped a U.S. flag over her.

A white-bearded chaplain commenced with the brief service. I felt myself breaking down, and focused on breathing. I squeezed Adam's hand, and thought more about my close friends who had come from out of state, re-scheduled

their own lives at the last minute. I tried not to think of Lee
Ann and her fiancé, neither of whom would talk to anyone,
Lee Ann never adjusting the stone face at the funeral when
I looked her way as I gave the eulogy. My immediate family
was truly gone. As amazing as my social and love life had be-
come, something about this total loss of family drained me.

At some point, the chaplain asked that I come up to
collect the flag. I complied, not knowing what to expect.
Within the quiet woods, the four men who carried Abby
on their shoulders folded the flag. Their precision and care
conveyed love. Of course, they couldn't possibly know who
Abby really was, or understand what she meant to everyone
gathered there; I imagine they received a few lines about
the body they were carrying — her dates of service, which
branches of the military she called her own. They couldn't
know her, but given the ritual, it felt that they did. They understood our loss. When the leader presented the flag to me,
looking me straight in the eye to say *We appreciate what your
mother did for this country.* My jaw fell in a broken, muted sob.
I am critical of the military, but only its kinder aspects were
shown in this ritual. The raw fabric of the triangular flag
meant something to me. It showed that Abby mattered. That
she was seen. That the sacrifices in her life had not been for
naught. I felt overwhelming gratitude at this gesture, and I
brought the flag close to my chest. Its stars reminding me
of so much: where I could imagine her soul to be now; the
midnight stars of the Alaskan state flag; our naive and hero-
ic ambitions, captured so well near the end of *The Aeneid:
Opta ardua pennis sequi astra. They choose hardship who follow
the stars.* Having the military's appreciation in tangible form,
having our journey in tangible form — my chest heaved.

I returned to my seat. My sister scoffed. I didn't look at
her directly, but I felt her eyes bearing into me. She wanted
me to know that she thought I was ridiculous. She wanted me to know that my display of grief was just that — a

display. She wanted me to know that I did not belong here. I was not man enough for the military, by temperament, ability, or choice. She wanted me to know that I could not understand the meaning of any of this. And for the first time in my life, I knew her judgment to be hopelessly invalid.

I didn't flinch at the rifle shots. Someone shrieked, and we all laughed. I knew Mom would have loved that shriek. When pressed with the terrifying, she hoped everyone would laugh.

The funeral director was a kind woman in her mid-40s whose hair reminded me of Miss Frizzle, the eccentric teacher from *The Magic School Bus*. She told us to give them 15 minutes before the burial. It felt like we were VIPs at a restaurant, on the verge of enjoying a terribly large and fattening cake. If she had children, they probably were in middle school. I wondered aloud to a friend if the director ever volunteered at Career Day. We laughed in the car. She had brought me Chambord. We drank it straight in Solo cups and toasted to Abby.

Most people left after the military ceremony, including Lee Ann. They did not see the coffin get attached to a crane. They did not see it lowered into the ground. By men in yellow construction outfits, lowered with gentleness and care, but in the same motions as workers pouring concrete for a sidewalk. "It's hitting me now," one of Abby's close friends said with a sharp cry. The wind sliced at us with greater force. There was no point in watching this. It was just pain. Like her gasping for breath, that "air hunger." Like seeing her in the final hours, her white-pupils crested in a black film, her frame skeletal, skin all bruised yellow or blue. I took photos of her then, as she did with Grandma. I thought the impulse to photograph a dead parent was a weird one. But now I understand.

I suggested we all get some comfort food somewhere. I put on a sociable face. My body could not convulse fast enough to match the grief anyway, so I accustomed myself to the cold weight of numbness.

The fact of my family gone pervades me. The force of my mother's abeyance is intolerable.

To attempt to speak of what has been, would be impossible. Abyss has no Biographer — Had it, it would not be Abyss.

I don't remember the drive from the funeral home to the burial site. I don't remember the drive to the post-burial restaurant. I still have yet to fathom that I will never drive with Mom again.

CHAPTER 19

Slug Bug

Several months after she passed, a man messaged me in the "Other" inbox of Facebook. He knew Abby in middle and high school. She was one of the sweetest people he'd ever met, a sentiment I'd see echoed by dozens of total strangers. But unlike the others, he told me something unexpected about Abby.

"Your Mom was great at fixing cars."

I replied incredulous. She always knew how to restart a cranky engine, change a tire, or check the oil, but I never considered this unusual. "Oh yeah," he typed in real-time. "She went to mechanic school for a while." I thanked this man for adding to all I knew of Abby: Sunday school teacher, water bottle entrepreneur, Marine Corps scarlet, and now, amateur mechanic.

What comes before you keeps adding up.

Abby's first car was an old Chevy Camaro. My parents owned a Ford Taurus then a Volkswagen Beetle, the existence of both bleeds into my early memories: the silver sheen of the Taurus; the white of the Volkswagen, a touch of rust, its rainbow sticker on the bumper, how we loved that movie with the "slug bug" that turns out to be alive.

CHAPTER 20

Sand Dollars

It's odd that I don't recall more of our trips to the beach. Canyon Country was a good 45 minutes from Santa Monica. An hour from Ventura. Both had public beaches, but we preferred Ventura for some reason. I more fondly recall driving to the beach than being on the beach. I liked passing the orange trees in Fillmore, the shacks selling candy and used clothes, coasting a hand out the window up and down.

Beaches have never been among my favorite locations, which I suppose makes me not a beach person. I want to be a beach person; the alternative doesn't seem much fun. But my memory betrays my posturing. I've always shown resistance to sand. Coming back from Ventura, I once volunteered to take out the trash if I could be the first to take a bath.

"Why do you want to be first so badly?" They asked.

"So I don't have to worry about your sand when I take a bath."

They couldn't stop laughing. Children can be selfish, so long as they're blunt and strategic about it.

In remembering the beach, what I most keenly recall has nothing to do with the beach: the Cheetos we snacked on, the belt of warm wind against our faces driving down there; the music we played (Radio Disney, Christian rock, The Dixie Chicks).

I wonder what the beach meant to Mom. Despite being in the Great Lakes region, Potterville was far away from any Great Lake. But Abby was content with the smaller lakes she rode her bike to. Perhaps the vastness of the sea fascinated her. The vivacity of waves must have been a welcome excitement from the small-town tedium of calm lakes. Just as

New York City gave me an energy not found in Alaska, perhaps the ocean gave her similar vitality.

We'd wade into the waves. I believe my babysitter let me see *Jaws* when I was seven, so I never ventured out that far. That I wouldn't go far out in the water disappointed my father, an avid scuba diver. But Mom was cool watching me pretend to be a turtle. I lay belly-down on a boogie board, paddling with my palms, going a great distance in my mind.

I don't recall talking with her on the beach, as much as being with her under the sun, her watching as I built sandcastles and hummed to myself, her turning half her attention back to a medical or legal thriller. She always kept carrots and cans of root beer in a red cooler. She packed Oreos, and when I was lucky, Reese's.

I have a clear memory of us on a boating trip off Ventura. She was homeschooling me, so I was about 10, and she was about 37. She signed me up for more extracurriculars in the hope I'd make some friends. The lesson was something about marine biology — the kids visited an aquarium, placed their hands on furry sea anemones. We rode out to sea on a drab yacht. It took us out to view reclusive sea lions. We heard their barks through a howling wind. The waves were choppy. Adults told us to stay away from the railing. I fidgeted with the buckle of my life jacket to make sure it truly was fastened. I considered an errant bump in the ocean, sending us all overboard. Or only me jettisoned into the ocean. As everyone sped away, I'd cry out. They'd be gone soon enough, and I'd fend for myself as the sharks circled (fucking *Jaws*).

I felt calmer knowing Mom was on board. Not so much that she could save me, but that there was someone on the ship who would notice my absence. Did I think what would happen should she be tossed overboard? I doubt it. The possibility of her death was too remote, as unthinkable and earth-destroying as gravity flicked off.

Around eight, I used to play a mortality game with deflating balloons leftover from family celebrations — I'd bounce the crinkling balloon atop my head in the living room: as many bounces as I got was how many years Mom and I would live together. I got to something like 939 once. At 10, were she to go overboard, I would have screamed and screamed, but I don't think I would have jumped after her. As a man, I wouldn't hesitate to jump from any height to save her. I'd much rather risk drowning together than her going off alone. I'll always regret not thinking to read her *Love You Forever*, the children's book Robert Munsch wrote after losing two children. The refrain was a lullaby that played in his head for years — he couldn't sing it without crying, so he wrote it down:

> *I'll love you forever,*
> *I'll love you for always,*
> *As long as I'm living*
> *My baby you'll be.*

In the book, this is what the mother sings to her son as an infant, teenager, young man, middle-aged man. Then she has white hair and gets all hunched over (Abby never got to wear her hair in a white bun); he sneaks up to her room and rocks her with love, not to sleep, as they're already sleeping, but in an acting love beyond consciousness. The son sings his inherited song:

> *I'll love you forever,*
> *I'll love you for always,*
> *As long as I'm living*
> *My mother you'll be.*

I always thought when the time came, I would muster such strength, dignity, courage. Lord knows I tried. But I didn't sing her that song when the time came.

She loved sand dollars. I did too. We walked around the beach collecting sand dollars.

CHAPTER 21

Paulie

In the summer of 1998, Mom drove me to meet an avian vet. Several months earlier, I had seen the movie *Paulie*, about a lonely, blue-crowned conure with the gift of gab. The conure tells his life's story to a happy-go-lucky janitor, who sympathizes with the loss of an irreplaceable friendship with Marie, a girl about my age.

All it took was 10 minutes with *Paulie* for birds to capture my imagination. The look of them, the feel of them, their possibility of flight. They flew through my dreams. I started to print out pictures of Scarlet macaws, doves, and love birds. I got to over 60 pages when my dad told me to cool it with the printer. "Hate to inform you buddy, but color ink is super expensive." I didn't mind the injunction. I already had plenty of 8x11 images to work with. With a hand-held hole punch, I punched the computer paper, trying to keep it all aligned. I strung the mottled pages together with a different colored string. If I wanted more of one species in the front, or more action shots later on, I unpeeled the cut-out, moved as needed, and re-glued. I suppose that untitled bird book was my first foray into content curation, graphic design, and publishing.

Mom learned of the bird book, and decided to encourage my interest, which taken to the extreme, wouldn't make the worst profession in the world. The avian vet was, I suppose, a respectable enough fantasy. I always struggled with what to be on career day. I told the adults what I sensed they wanted to hear: firefighter or astronaut. These were masculine and highly-praised endeavors. Playing doctor was also acceptable, and one of my favorite videos with Abby is me around five placing a stethoscope on her chest.

"Breath in," my high voice commands. She does so emphatically.

"Breath in," I repeat.

She plays along, even when I place the stethoscope on her forehead.

I really wanted to be an actor, but my bones knew that could never be. My father disdained "liberal Hollywood." Acting wasn't real work. In his world, being gay was disappointing enough, but being an actor — that was just unconscionable.

The vet's office was on Wilshire Boulevard. I recognized the famous street from the disaster flick, *Volcano*. I was more impressed by the length and beauty of Wilshire Boulevard than the actual offices Abby took me to. One doctor was a middle-aged white guy, dry as beef-jerky, who seemed to regret every instant spent with me.

The younger one was Korean and took a greater interest. He showed me around his office – the rows of reference books fascinated me – the possibility of holding all that knowledge, knowing how to use those fat books as sources, to think and move through the world like a sorcerer. The vet showed me a few of the birds he was caring for. He gave me the smallest strap glove he had, which went past my elbow. He placed a giant cockatoo on my left arm. I had always imagined birds as light, aerial creatures; their sloppy weight surprised me. My right arm came to support my left. "You can pet him if you'd like," the doctor encouraged.

With great hesitation, I lightly stroked the back of the cockatoo's skull. He tolerated it for a few seconds, before shaking me away. I tried stroking the side of his chest with a pointer finger. He snapped at me, a bit lazy, but a clear warning. I flinched so badly my left arm fell like a snapped rope bridge. The cockatoo leapt up to fly away. He perched atop a cage across the room. The doctor laughed. My eyes shined terror. The first vet had warned me that you had to be okay with some scratches and bites. "Some macaws, if they really want to bite you, can cut through the bone."

The good doc ushered me into another room. He said a lot of hard work and patience went into becoming a veterinarian, but I could do it. Over time, you'd know how to read what animals would do next. "It really is all about hard work. If you're passionate about it, you should go for it."

Seeing how the cockatoo behaved, noting that it was about half the size of a Scarlet macaw, a species that at nearly three-feet tall could probably cleave in half the finger of an eight-year-old, my career as an avian vet ended.

Where was Mom during all these tours through vet offices? On the sidelines, watching. Encouraging me. She beamed whenever someone complimented me, or encouraged me, especially when the odds weren't stacked in my favor.

She never liked drawing attention to herself. Though now, I wish she had, and in writing this I suppose I am requesting that she speak up. She is worthy of being the center of focus. She is welcome – needed – in these memories. We want her to speak. We long for her voice.

But perhaps, like me, she prefers acting at a distance. She'd rather help than be helped, talk of others than of self. It's a relatively noble impulse – this lack of selfishness – but it requires a counterweight. Can one know or respect one's self without a little degree of selfishness? There is a need to put one's self out there. To enter reality, act, and accept the consequences. I gave up the idea of being an avian vet as soon as I encountered the reality of the avian species. Did that abandonment of a goal simply recapitulate a habit of not fighting to make one's love happen? I still have trouble accepting compliments. When my thoughts are unique and valuable, more often than not, I do not speak up. Being great at something requires the strangulation of so many other dreams; and there is never a guarantee of success. At times, it seems best never to make a move you can't take back.

It's a battle we both faced: being fully at the center of the story, and accepting whatever consequences are tied to the beginning and middle, accepting that there always has to be an end.

CHAPTER 22

Kaladi

I took her to Kaladi Brothers on Old Seward Highway. It was sunny for late September. She loved the orange walls inside, smooth as mango. I climbed the step from the parking lot without thought or effort. She shuffled to the ramp. She nearly tripped on the slight step up to it. It may have been half an inch tall. It all suddenly hit then: your mother is dying.

The decline – the moments where death was unmistakably approaching – was relatively quick. Five days when it all became inescapable: this is really happening.

I recently finished Jayson Greene's memoir about the sudden death of his two-year-old girl, *Once More We Saw Stars*. I wondered if the parents were lucky not to see a decline. Or would they have preferred it? More time to say goodbye, but more time to watch their loved one vanish second by second. Look into their dimming eyes.

My sister flew up on a Saturday. I came home, which was the apartment I was sharing with Abby in South Anchorage, at 3am after a night with friends. I should have suspected something was seriously wrong when Mom stopped responding around 10pm. But I was out. It was Saturday. I was having fun. She probably was sleeping.

I will never forgive myself for not rushing home once Mom stopped texting, or rather, started texting random symbols. They were all happy symbols, even if together they made a disconcerting paragraph. Mom was a goofy person. I told myself she was just being goofy. This was an easier narrative to buy; it made me more comfortable.

Lee Ann would exploit this once we became enemies.

"If you're such a great caretaker, where the hell were you when Mom was on the floor for hours?" Her voice rose over mine. Abby was in her last days, and we were arguing about moving Abby back home, or keeping her in the hospital. "Where were you — you little shit?"

I ignored her and bypassed the reality: I was getting drunk with friends and flirting with strangers.

I could have asked her the same. I didn't, because I was the peacemaker. I always was the peacemaker. I, like Mom, had to be because Lee Ann, like Dad, never said sorry. I didn't ask why in the last eleven months she had visited Abby only twice, cutting both visits short, treating the last as a vacation for her new fiancé and his 11-year-old daughter ("She really wants to see a sled dog race," Lee Ann told me repeatedly. "It's pretty adorable how into dogs she is."). I didn't ask why she didn't contribute a cent to Mom's food or rent, or why she told her to go on an "all green diet" and replace chemo with supplements and smoothies. She'd likely yell at me in retort — "What the fuck are you talking about! I paid to have those shipped up here. They were super fucking expensive ok. We're talking thousands of dollars I contributed!" (The boxes of supplements were $1,200 total. I saw on the receipt, as I was the one who picked up all the boxes, who made all the disgusting concoctions, who will always hear a UPS clerk say to her boss when it was clear the recipient couldn't make it, "This man's mother allegedly has cancer." When I told Lee Ann, she replied with, "Well, what do you expect. Those boxes are valuable.")

"Huh? If you think it's such a grand fucking idea to take her home where you'll have to be the one to bathe her and give her medicine, where if she slips and breaks a hip it'll be all your fault, then do whatever the hell you want. But don't come crying to me when you can't help her. Where were you when you had to call the firefighters to lift her off the goddamn floor?"

I told her Abby wanted to pass at home. Jeremy, who was rapidly coming back into the picture during her illness, had also heard Abby say that she didn't want to die in a hospital. As her husband, he had the most authority on whether she would be released to hospice, and he planned on signing the release.

But Lee Ann wasn't having it, and she loudly proclaimed her disagreement. I only spoke of Abby's wishes. It wasn't the place to defend myself. I did not ask Lee Ann where was she to make those green-brown smoothies, to see Abby's scrunched face cough up the protein powder; where was she to sit next to Abby in an infusion chair, or read to her for an hour before sleep. Lee Ann made thrice as much as me and lived 2,000 miles closer to Abby. Yet I was the one going up every six weeks, who was there the last month to make her food, watch *Blue Bloods* and *Military Wives*, massage her feet; I was the one to see her stare into space for hours, becoming a skeleton; I was the one to rephrase what the doctor said into, as Abby wanted, a more hopeful forecast; I was the one to crack jokes about chained penguins as we hobbled through a parking lot, weak from another appointment.

When Lee Ann was through security at LAX, I texted to ask if she could get a taxi to the hospital. Mom was weak. I feared she could pass any second.

"Are you kidding me?" She texted back. "I'm about to take off and you're springing this shit on me now? You need to call me. Now."

Lee Ann seems so much like a villain in these renderings. I wish they were false. For most of my life, I have told myself Lee Ann is fundamentally a good person. Even when her actions were evil, I worked hard to tell myself otherwise.

I called her, opening with a plea to order her a Lyft.

She refused. "I can't believe you're pulling this shit on me. I don't know this airport I'm coming to. I don't know Anchorage. You can't just spring this on me. If you can't pick me up, I'm not coming. You need to tell me now if you're not picking me up because I will not board this plane if you're going to backslide on your promise of picking me up. You told me you were going to pick me up."

I thought about how, from 15 on, Lee Ann had visited Mom several summers and winters, and more recently during her illness. She knew the airport. This would hardly be her first time in Alaska. I thought back to finding Abby on the bedroom floor at 3am. I tried to move her to a chair, or back to bed. She kept muttering about wanting to turn off a light. I couldn't move her. No one ever tells you how difficult it is to move an adult body, especially a fragile one you fear breaking. The best I got was to lean her against a chair. Half an hour later, I grew frustrated. Mom kept muttering to leave her be.

"You really can't get up," I said, my voice blending scorn, pity, and sad fact.

"I can't get up," she said simply.

I was exhausted. I didn't know who to call. It was after 4am. My heart broke.

"Why don't we try to sleep a little," I said, finally.

"Yes," she breathed.

I covered her in a blanket. I grabbed myself a pillow and slept near her on the floor. A little after 8am, I woke. Mom was in the same position, leaning against a couch, her head nesting in the nook between the couch and the wall.

"Good morning wonderful Mother," I greeted her. "Wanna try standing up again? Then I can make us some pancakes."

"In a bit," she smiled weakly. "In a bit."

Her arms were twitching. Her jaw seemed slackened too far to the right. I worried she had a stroke. Only then did it enter my mind that I could call 911.

"Sounds like you need a lifting service" the dispatcher explained. "I'll send some firefighters over." I told Mom some hot firefighters were heading over to help us. She laughed, weakly.

The firefighters brought paramedics. I said she had late-stage cancer. In between their nods and note-taking, I found myself saying she was a former Marine, a lively person who loved to travel, is normally super friendly. "If she were well, she'd be offering you all snacks right now." They took this in. Graciously, I see in retrospect. How many frantic relatives they must have met, each telling them quick stories of their loved one now confined. What vain hope: to make a stranger feel all that someone means to you with just a couple of stories.

Mom perked up with six people surrounding her on the floor. Two on each side helped lift her. Seeing the ease of her ascent, I thought Oh. That's how you do it. Two people. Had Lee Ann been there, we could have helped her.

I decided to capitulate, and pick up Lee Ann. Abby would want to see her; that was my number one reason. Then came the typical justifications: Lee Ann was stressed over missed work, she feared not seeing Mom before she passed, she was afraid of death. With a cold fate bearing down on us, raw responses came out. The question remains whether such reactions are one's true character magnified, or portraits distorted beyond fairness.

From Providence Hospital to Ted Stevens International Airport, I sped in Matey across town. I would never forgive Lee Ann if Mom died in the hospital while I was picking her up from the airport. With Jeremy watching over Abby, I high-tailed it through a black Alaskan morning a bit after 4am on a Sunday. I wondered if Lee Ann had always been a tyrant or had become one over the years. Others simply did not enter her top considerations. With the hospice question, she kept repeating that as a police officer, she couldn't be connected with any faulty homecare. Were Abby discharged then hurt in our care, that could reflect very poorly on her. Lee Ann demanded that Abby be sent to a hospice house. The nurses explained this wasn't an option in Alaska, which only had mobile hospice nurses, given the state's size.

"Then she should stay in the hospital," Lee Ann repeated.

"But that's not what she wants," I repeated.

"Then I don't know what to tell you. I can't be held responsible if she trips in the bathroom and breaks a hip. I just can't have that on my record." Abby at this point couldn't move her fingers.

Lee Ann certainly did not consider anything I had been through in the last 24 hours. Once the paramedics secured Abby in a wheelchair, I followed the ambulance to Providence. My wide eyes focused on the van, its blue-red lights swirling, no siren. I stared at the vehicle carrying Mom, wishing her safe from any bumps, wanting to scream at the city for halting traffic on one street for construction, forcing us into divots that jolted us up and down. And now I see this procession foreshadowed the funeral, which would move over us in just two weeks.

Lee Ann's flight was delayed an hour. Jeremy texted me that Abby was alright. I figured I should make Lee Ann comfortable. I should embrace her. She was my sister. We were from the same mother.

I greeted Lee Ann in smile. For the sake of this trip, I'd pretend that all was forgiven. She did the same by not mentioning my near supposed dereliction of duty.

It was before 6am. In the spirit of a vague tradition, I suggested we catch breakfast at Denny's. I forget what we talked about. Mostly gentler memories of our "crazy" adventures in Alaska — mostly featuring Victoria, or that time Mom yelled "I can't take it anymore!" on a family road trip and ran full-speed into the wilderness. Lee Ann did not ask how I was holding up. I told her about the unpleasantries Mom had faced — the morning on the floor (how gleefully she'd use this against me) and the MRI scan. When Abby and I arrived in the ER, the doctor, with limited knowledge of Abby's situation, thought the cancer had spread to her brain. To confirm would require a brain scan. While logical, I could not in the moment process how stupid this was. Abby was just over 100 pounds. Looking at photos of her then, I am surprised I wasn't more fearful; she was so clearly close to death. I suppose I had been with her through the changes and wasn't as shocked by the transformation as those who hadn't seen her in a week or two. And my love for her, as her love for me, was always greater than fear.

The doctor was young. Both her parents were probably still living. Perhaps she had never had a close relative die. Either way, quality of life did not factor into her decision.

"The good news," she informed the room, "Is that we can use her port. So no needles."

Mom just smiled. She was delirious. Her body counterbalanced the toxins flowing into her body with endorphins. Abby had seen this fate play out with Victoria, the breakdown of the body, both bad and good released, the return of a childish state of wonder, innocence and coziness with the world, a last-minute, graceful giddiness sent from the body. I wish I had known enough to tell the doctor no, just let her continue in this natural delirium.

We wheeled her downstairs. The nurse had helped her change, and placed her supine on a stretcher. The nurse was dark blonde, stern-looking, brisk, the popular type who played volleyball at my high school.

In the basement, a Paul Rudd character greeted us. He said it got noisy in there. They could put headphones on and play music. Would she like that?

"Oh, that's very nice." My voice was earnest, with pleasantness tacked on for Mom. "She'd love that." I suggested "This Kiss" by Faith Hill, the EP I got her when I was 11, the one she played in the Mustang on repeat. The procedure would take 20 minutes. They asked me to wait in a nearby room.

I felt some guilt for how relieved I was for a break. I called Lee Ann while Abby got the CT scan. I told her yes, it wasn't looking good; she should get on the next flight out of LA. She thanked me for being there for Mom. I said of course, and turned back to Mom. Lee Ann's gratitude never sunk in. Perhaps I thought it wasn't genuine. Or maybe I didn't believe that at this point I could be a good son; good sons, for starters, don't let their mothers die.

That phone call was one of the closest moments I felt to Lee Ann. We were in this together, something I hadn't felt since Thanksgiving 2016, shortly after Mom's scare with sepsis (A stitch in her colon done in Chicago wasn't all that sturdy – "Oh Matthew, I thought that was it." Abby told me. "I thought I was going."). We had all raced to Alaska. As Mom recovered, we reminisced and bought her presents — owl socks, cute purses, brushes with thick monochromatic handles. Now, with Mom peacefully getting an MRI, Lee Ann was saying we would get through this together. I nearly cried with relief. Finally! Finally someone to help like family. I would not have to go at this all alone.

Nurse Volleyball returned. "Sorry to interrupt. Could you come in here. We're having a problem."

I told Lee Ann I had to go, that I loved her, and I'd see her soon at the airport.

"Love you too *bradour*," she said with a joking lilt, "See you soon. Stay strong."

I followed Nurse Volleyball toward a gargantuan MRI machine. Abby lay prone in it, diminished in its bulk. I had entered a sci-fi movie; this was the opening scene where I learn that aliens have captured my mother.

"We can't get her to stay still," Nurse Volleyball told me. "I already gave her some mood stabilizers, but that hasn't helped."

(If only I knew that these "stabilizers" would render Abby speechless for the next several hours, that the childlike sentences she could make before the hospital would be too soon obliterated. Great God — if only I knew.)

"Could you go up to her and maybe talk a bit about something that will keep her calm. Then I'll give her another dosage and see if that helps."

I forget what I said to Nurse Volleyball. I was struck by how mechanical she talked. She spoke of Abby as she would a car, all within earshot. My memory cuts suddenly to stroking Abby's arms. Her eyelids were fluttering shut and open. I brushed her hair. I gave a gentle massage to her temples, which were clamped by two cold braces. Nurse Volleyball said the procedure would re-commence shortly. I said thank you. She left without so much as a nod.

I spoke loudly to Abby. I had to get through the fog of drugs.

I love you so much…
    You're doing great…
        It'll all be worth it…
            It's like a spaceship, no?…

I'm right nearby, ok.
I'm not going anywhere…
I love you more than anything…

Paul Rudd spoke through the speaker. Were we ready?

I looked down at Mom. She looked rested, considering the inhospitable setting. I gave the thumbs up. Paul Rudd came out behind the glass to prep her.

"Could you stand in the technician booth? I think we'll be able to get a clean read now, but in case we need you."

"Of course, no problem."

From behind the glass, I saw him move her body into the machine's circumference. It was jarring to see her so abruptly and mechanically handled, then left alone. He joined me in the control room.

"Okay Abby," he spoke softly into, from what I understood, her headphones. "You're going to hear some music your son, Matthew, picked out for you, then we're going to start. You're going to hear some loud noises. Do your best to keep still. If you can keep still, we can get a good read and all of this will be over in 15 minutes." Were she well, I imagine she'd respond chipper and stoic, like a pilot from *JAG*, the legal military-melodrama from the 90s. She'd accept this unpleasant mission, perhaps saying something corny like, "Let's ride."

The boom shook me. Like all psych students, I learned about CTs and MRIs, but no book had ever mentioned just how loud an MRI was. I now google "MRI noise" to find headlines like, "MRIs are NOISY!" and explanations: "The banging is the vibration of metal coils in the machine caused by rapid pulses of electricity." To see my weak mother in that alien machine sapped my strength, but to see her immediate reaction to the booming noise destroyed me.

She shook her head violently. Her hands, ostensibly weak, moved toward the head brace. She continued thrashing as she tried to remove the clamps. She looked tortured. I have yet to experience a comparable shock. This was to watch my mother electrocuted.

Maybe 20 seconds passed.

"Whoa'k," Paul Rudd sounded disappointed. "This isn't going to work. Could you go to her. We need photos of the head, obviously, but you could touch her feet. Maybe that will help."

I did as told.

I removed her headphones. I kissed her forehead. I spoke to her loudly.

> Mom you're doing great...
> > Mom. I'm so sorry this is happening....
> > > We're gonna get through this...
> > > > They're letting me stay here with you...

Her feet were facing me as the machine drew her back in. I didn't let go of her feet and walked with the moving body tray. I smiled. I stood on my tiptoes for her to see me. If magnetism 60,000 times stronger than the earth's core was about to run through her mind, then I would beam a force to counter it (Oh Abby, you gave me so much faith in the power of vain hope and love). I wore earmuffs. The terrible noises began. I broke out into song.

Over a decade ago, Mom and I ventured to the Alaska State Fair. We went every year. Each time, I asked if she'd go on one of the smaller rides with me. She always said no; they scared her.

"C'mon" I prodded. "Even the baby ones?"

"Even the baby ones."

But I think it was 2005 when my 15-year-old self somehow convinced Abby to join me on a ride. It was a carousel situation, but one that bopped up and down, two to a seat, a slender bar holding us in. I was thrilled that Mom was about to brave her baseless fear of rides, that after this, she'd discover they really weren't so bad, and from here on out, she would always be my riding buddy. Sensing my happiness, Abby smiled through her terror. As the seats rose up quickly 20 feet, I realized I had made a grave mistake.

"Oh my God oh my God," her voice rose with panic. Like most teenagers, I thought my parents were unbreakable against any challenge — when things really mattered, there wasn't a force greater than them. "Oh Jesus. Oh Lord." She clutched her chest. She looked around for the nonexistent exit. She gripped the outside rim of the seat, then the flimsy bar belt. Uncontrollably, nonsensically, she felt that she was going to die.

I gripped her hand. "Mom are you alright?"

The ride shot forward, and she yelped. Terror had replaced her. I hugged her close to me. She cried uncontrollably in what I now know to be a panic attack. "Stop the ride" I yelled. But the seasonal high school employee was sealed in his glass booth and didn't hear me, or, given the lengthy line, chose to ignore my plea. So around we went, flung up and down, Mom clinging to me, me saying, "It'll be over soon." The song just came to me. "This little light of mine," I sang into her ear. "I'm gonna let it shine. This little light of mine, I'm gonna let it shine —." She sang with me, shaken and terrified the whole ride. I sang louder. "Won't let Satan blow it out, I'm gonna let it shine." She sang with me. It seemed to diminish her agony. It reminded her that a higher power stood over this pain, that even as mortal jaws opened, a larger power loomed capable of shutting up hell.

I rubbed her drugged legs as I shouted "This little light of mine! I'm gonna let it shine!" Her face grimaced. She twitched her head. But she did not thrash. At least for several minutes.

I switched to another Christian song. "He set me free." It was our favorite song back in Sylmar. In retrospect, probably not the best song to chant when one is confined in an MRI machine. She was nearly calm for another minute. Then she started thrashing. I sang louder, to no effect. Her writhing and muted scowls were too much for me. This was a woman who loved horses. Her favorite memories as a child were riding her bike and swimming in the lake. In the past year, she had found energy to walk outside each day, taking photos of flowers, bees, the sunrise. This was not a soul to confine.

I turned around to Paul Rudd. "Stop it please" I said loudly. The machine continued. She moved more wildly. I turned directly to face him. He wasn't looking at us. I walked to him, waving both arms. "I think we can stop now!" I shouted. He didn't look up. My fist banged on the glass. He looked up. I screamed: "Stop this machine right now!"

When Lee Ann asked me to pick her up from the airport, Mom hadn't been through the MRI. She had not yet declined at an unbelievably rapid rate. Before the MRI, I had agreed to pick up Lee Ann from the airport. But 18 hours later, our mother was on the threshold of death.

"Plans change," I told Lee Ann. "I don't want to leave Mom."

"That's just like you to go back on what you promised." She replied. "Why can't you see that you are breaking your promise."

When I did pick Lee Ann up from the airport, she showed no consideration for what Mom and I had been through. She asked the names of local gyms, and if anyone could drive her there at least once a day. We split all lunches and dinners. The mass shooting in Las Vegas at a country music festival would eventually claim all her attention; she'd talk over and over again about friends of friends who were near the scene of the crime. She was not willing to spend the night at the hospital. "Let Jeremy do it," she rational-

ized. "They're husband and wife." She seemed eager to take
any path that required her to think of Mom less.

Despite Lee Ann's fierce resistance, Abby was set to
leave the hospital on Monday afternoon and return home.
That morning, Lee Ann and I had our final spate. She wanted to go someplace good for breakfast after she worked out.
Lee Ann claimed she wanted to go back to the hospital, but
all her actions suggested that she was in no hurry. Her triv-
iality and rampant selfishness were corroding my patience.
But that she felt no urgency to be with our mother, who
could die at any second, was the last straw. I was short with
her. I asked if she really needed to work out this morning.
She curtly replied, "Well then when the hell should I work
out."

I inhaled sharply. "Lee Ann — just give me some space
for a bit."

Lee Ann was never capable of withstanding any criticism
or sentiment less than laudatory. She went nuclear.

"Oh, I'm sorry. Are my simple questions bothering you.
What, you need your space huh? You need a safe space?
What, should I just get a hotel? Is that what you want me
to do?"

I looked at this woman I had defended my entire life.
I hated those kids who criticized her growing up. When an
uncle said she was selfish, I stopped speaking to him for days.
As a five-year-old in karate, I went berserk on a kid who
said something mean to my sister; that was a story she frequently told: "He just jumped on this kid who was like, four
years older than him, and started beating the shit out of him.
It was nuts. He went all full-out psycho helping me."

Growing up, she always claimed that she was the one
to defend me because everyone thought I was weird. But
the truth was, I never saw her defend me. She had no real
interest in acting like a sister to me. As adults, the birthday
presents I sent her were never reciprocated. In our quarterly

phone calls, it was always about herself. She had met Adam several times and asked him no more than two questions. She was a narcissist. Through and through. It had never been so undeniable as now.

I looked directly into her eyes. "Yeah, I think that's a good idea."

She was shocked. I had never, when there were actual consequences, rebuffed her. When she got like this, I was always the one to recompose myself into whatever configuration she needed. But not now. We were on equal footing now. And equality is unacceptable for people who think they're the center of the universe.

"Okay wow. Fine. You don't want me here, fine. I'll get a hotel. You really have some nerve. I didn't think I'd have to get a hotel. I'm going to have to spend a lot of money. Then I have to get a car now, and —."

The predictable tantrums followed. But I'd rather she explicitly be out of the way and angry at me, than watch her half-hearted help that only brought everyone down.

I know her discontentment, her disgruntlement, her anger — it didn't all stem from me. I was closer to Abby. By all objective measures, I was the "better" child. Not that Abby saw or felt that way, but that was what everyone around us observed. Lee Ann, as self-centered as she could be, noticed. I had done everything I could to comfort Abby. Perhaps Lee Ann, now seeing that the end was approaching faster than she had thought, wished she had done more. That may explain some of her anger. I hope so. I hope she feels that she could have done more. Otherwise, I am unjustifiably defending her again. I am, yet again, hoping to believe she's a good person when all her actions suggest otherwise.

I only saw Lee Ann a few more times. Toward the end, as Abby's body gasped for air, I tried to make peace.

"I know you hate me right now," I prefaced my appeal. "But I'm glad you're here." She glared at me. Then exploded,

"I'm done with you. Seriously. I don't ever want to talk to you again." That she spat this out two feet from our dying mother will always amaze me. "Sounds great," I said, moving back to the other side of Abby's bed. "I'm perfectly fine with that."

Whenever she was in the apartment those last hours, I tried to ignore our tension. I ignored her disgusted face when I recited an anecdote or sang to Mom. I played diplomat when she took a necklace I had placed in Abby's line of vision. I had bought the necklace on H Street, at Octopus Ink, a boutique store in downtown Anchorage. I was 21, and working at the front desk of the nearby Hilton. For Mother's Day, I wanted to get her something special, so I scrounged up $50 for a necklace with an iron dove silhouette at the center – doves being among her favorite beings – with five red pebbles strewn around the dark-gilt chain.

"Oh, look at that," Lee Ann said, placing the necklace around herself, locking it before I could object. "Here's the necklace I bought Mom."

I breathed in deeply. I knew some lawyers; I would do whatever was necessary to get that necklace back. I wouldn't confront Lee Ann here. She was a ticking bomb. She'd start yelling at me if I suggested that I had bought the necklace, which was the last sound Mom deserved to hear.

Lee Ann wore the necklace for another hour or two. Bored with Mom's bedside, she roved the apartment that she had not contributed a dime to. She came across a drawing pad marked "Drawing is Therapy" in bright colors. I had found it at the Cooper-Hewitt Design Museum in Manhattan and sent it to Abby who drew dozens of colored drawings I now cherish. Lee Ann flipped through these sketches, smiling at times. I knew near the end, she'd come across a drawing of that necklace. It was dated June 1, 2017. In light blue-purple colored pencil, Mom wrote at the bottom right: Sketches of the necklace Matthew gave me :)"

I waited to see how Lee Ann would react.

It's still hard to believe that she started to rip the drawing out.

"Please don't do that," I said.

It's not an exaggeration to say she snarled, "Why?"

"Because I bought that for Mom, and as you can see, I also got her that necklace, so if you could return both, that'd be great."

"Oh." She said, thinking. Perhaps plotting; a part of me looks at this abhorrent action fondly — the cop caught red-handed. "Oh," she repeated. There was manufactured disgust in her voice, as if to remind her that I was the dirty one here.

"Sure. I must have bought her another necklace." She unclasped it, tossed it my way with scorn.

I knew even then that her spite, as unwarranted as it was, had a clear origin. She knew she never gave Mom a necklace. She was being confronted with all that she did not do. I was a reminder of her regret. And, as was her habit, she'd rather attack the truth than accommodate it.

Once the hospice papers went through, I rushed to South Anchorage to make room for the incoming bed, something I understood to be heated and with varying inflation to prevent bedsores. I ran to Fred Meyer – buying candles, lotions, stuffed animals – anything possibly comforting.

The apartment was mostly ready when Abby came in on a stretcher. She looked confused. Or overwhelmed. Or perhaps she knew exactly what was going on; or perhaps she knew nearly nothing, as they gave her extra drugs for the bumpy road back from the hospital. I welcomed her home.

I am almost positive it was only me, maybe a friend or two helping me unpack groceries, setting up the handicap toilet Abby never used.

She started to cry. Her face was expressive but restricted, an open-mouthed wonder that could mean anything. A tear torrented down her cheek. At the time, I thought that she was so grateful to be back home, that her wishes were followed, that she literally cried. But weeks after she passed, I wondered if she was instead mourning the truth. She had returned home to die. The doctors, alas, could do no more. Hospice had come. It's a bit sad that the last interpretation seems most likely. Either way, it would have been better to have Lee Ann there. She is Abby's daughter. What would have happened had she been there to welcome her home?

CHAPTER 23

Travels

There's no right way to grieve. Have I always believed this? I must have heard this cliché after Victoria died. But that knowledge didn't take to my bones. Only after Abby passed did I realize that truth. There is no right or proper or correct or best way to grieve. It is a tragedy that we can only understand our parents' pain later in life, most often only once they're gone.

Weeks after her death, I tried returning eggs to a CVS in Manhattan. I was certain I had picked up a carton with two eggs missing and another cracked open, the yolk mysteriously missing. I was as certain of this as I was that the capital of California is Sacramento. I fought with the staff for recognition that I deserved a refund. Not until a manager showed me footage on his phone did I realize that the story I believed so passionately was wrong. I can't begrudge the manager with his clip-on tie from smiling as the evidence showed me grabbing another box entirely dissimilar to the one I claimed to have purchased there. I knew from grief memoirs that a loss of such magnitude precludes clear thinking, but again, I could not feel that until it became my reality. In physics, two possibilities can co-exist forever so long as you never choose one; so long as you keep one decision always unknown, it always exists.

I went to Ireland spontaneously some six months after her death. I wanted to be in Dublin for several days, a city whose writers knew mortality, its greatest book – *Ulysses* – set in motion after the death of Stephen Dedalus' mother. Financially, the trip made no sense: I used credit cards; I had no one to stay with; I had no travel points or voucher signaling Hey You — Now's the time to fly! It upset Adam, that I could buy a ticket to Dublin one day then tell him casually over dinner just days before the plane took off. "It worries me that you can keep a secret this big for so long."

I understood his frustrations; none of it made sense, and I couldn't articulate why I was going. I told him I needed to clear my head. I couldn't admit to myself that I was traveling in mourning for Abby.

When the border guard asked why I was coming to Ireland, I replied "Just to walk around." And for five days, I did just that, thinking of how much Abby would love the cobblestone, the old cafes. I had the juiciest chicken at The Hairy Lemon, then fried chicken at a street fair near Whelan's. I dined by myself at Italian and French restaurants where the wait staff were Irish. I hooked up with someone near the contemporary art museum. My jaw dropped seeing rows of ancient books at The Long Room at Trinity College. I talked to a statue of Oscar Wilde. Saw the sun eclipse into the Liffey.

Only on a bus ride back from Dublin, seeing the fields that truly were emerald, taking photographs of a beauty Abby would never see, did I break down. There was no denying it: I had come here in despair. Someone I loved was gone.

I was impatient against Abby's own trips across America in the wake of Victoria's death. She was such a master of smiling past her grief that I could not register just how essential these erratic voyages were; I could not perceive the weight and meaning of her loss, and in truth, I was a coward against the possibility of her grief pouring out. I repeated all the good memories we all had, as if recitation excused the howls of grief; I thought there was something noble in being emotionally stalwart, and she, given all her indoctrinations on how not to be a bother, agreed: her public grief over the woman who was closest to her — her own mother — had been minimal.

I should have welcomed an implosion. I should have flown to her, held her, and encouraged those painful tears. Instead, I proved to be no saint. Far from it. I did not go to my grandmother's funeral, citing finals for graduate school; Abby, citing her strong objection to open caskets, also abstained. "We'll have our own service," she told me. I agreed. But then she got sick, and there was no time.

In her grief, she eventually traveled to me. Her trips, often given with only a day's notice, stressed me and Adam. They forced us to reschedule dinner dates, work happy hours, study sessions. We made up a bed for Abby in the living room of our railroad-style apartment with terribly squeaky floors; we slept with full bladders rather than risk the chance of crossing the living room at night and waking her.

One Sunday, I planned a Mets game for the three of us. Abby was living in New Hampshire and was to spend the weekend with us. She was to meet us on the Upper East Side, then we'd take the 7 train to Queens. She was a couple of hours late. She had trouble navigating — her cell wasn't actually charging in the rental car, etc. Months later, when I flipped through her phone in the hospital, I saw pictures of a fox twined through the grill of the car. I'd ask if she had hit a fox while driving to us. She played it off. "I just didn't want you to worry about me."

We got to Citi Stadium eventually. Not in the best of humor, a few innings late. Mom was uncommonly exhausted from the trip. Of course, none of us knew she was ill.

We climbed to our nose-bleed seats. Several white guys, apparently drunk, kept screaming profanities a few seats behind us. "Fuck him in the ass!" one jeered. "Tear his fucking dick off!" commanded another. They were disaffected idiots looking for a fight. After an inning, Abby stood up to face them. "Excuse me. I want you to know I don't appreciate that language." She gestured to the people sitting around them; I tugged at her sleeve. "There are families here trying to have a nice time. Could you please tone down your language."

This was what they were waiting for. "Excuse me, but maybe I don't appreciate that you don't appreciate my language," one mocked.

I pulled Mom's sleeve down. "Ignore them, they're just idiots. They're looking for a fight."

After glaring at them for a few more seconds, she sat. Abby faced the field, keeping her head high and proud.

"Who brings their Mom to a baseball game?" one of them crackled.

Who doesn't, I thought.

We moved seats. Adam told a security guard who worked there, a bald CIA-looking fellow who happened to be a head honcho. He moved us right behind the diamond. I can only hope those guys were ejected. I cannot understand unnecessary cruelty; I've tried to, but that always seems to overlap with accepting it.

The new seats amazed Adam. He'd been watching The Mets play since he was a child, and he'd never been that close to the players. Mom smiled weakly. I sensed something was off, but I didn't press; she was just tired. That's what she told me later that night when I found the courage to ask. I couldn't tell you who the Mets were playing, whether they won or lost.

CHAPTER 24

Money

I sit on the private terrace of a luxury resort. This is the top floor of a hotel looking out on the beach for miles. The weather is warm but not overly hot; it's perfect for unthinking. Adam and I are in Florida for the wedding of one of his rich friends. I have trouble enjoying the manicured sand, the lounge chairs with their individual navy blue umbrellas. The cocktail servers roam around in mesh shoes. On the beach is a three-story restaurant, a fake Italian villa plastered in crème paint. The palm trees wave all content.

I keep thinking of the world's violence that creates such paradises. I think of Mom and Grandma; none of us could afford a vacation like this. I look up the etymology of *vacation*. The root word is *Vacare*, Latin for "to be unoccupied," and later the Middle English *Vacate*. None of us were ever unoccupied. Even Grandma in retirement found ways to volunteer or keep her social calendar packed. Our year-round 9-to-5s, for me and Mom, were never enough; we were always looking for small hustles. I passed through Mom's journals and felt crushed seeing how often she tabulated that week's bills; 10 days from her death, she was on the phone with AT&T to negotiate a late payment of $300. Our moments of respite came from reading books and watching TV, the democratized forms of entertainment; at times going to the movies — nothing extraordinary, just things beyond the stream of dull, constant work.

I sit on the patio of a luxury resort in Florida, writing without the red pen I have used for nearly all of this memoir; writing, instead, with a pen by Hilton. And when that ink becomes thick and unwieldy, I'll move on to a resort pen atop the expansive living room dresser.

These luxuries are restorative lifeblood to some of my new friends; the luxuries remind them of their childhoods. But they discomfort me. For Grandma, then Mom, then me, what we found comforting was something far beyond this resort. It was the adventure of being together. And in our ostensible poverty, we were happier than most with their supposed wealth. I'm thankful for the pecuniary existence now, even as I wish to bring them both to the hotels I now frequent.

We made our own comforts. And in that self-creation we discovered something real and vital. We did not seek to consume the world. We sought to give. We were happier for it.

The one resort vacation my family took, if a thin motel with no elevator and ten blocks from the beach can be called a resort, was to Coronado. It was 1998. We went down to San Diego for the 4th of July weekend: Independence Day parades and fireworks that night from the nondescript rooftop; SeaWorld all day for Sunday. I don't recall the drive down there. I embrace the unmemory, as what we don't recall may carry as much insight as those memories we seem able to attain. The best approximation of that drive is the haze of driving for hours along the highways of LA, fastened in by miles of brick wall flying along the white and yellow lines. I recall my furtive glances into other cars. We likely listened to Jimmy Buffet or The Beach Boys, anything to unwind Dad. He accepted the pose that Mom had no opinions on what should play in the car he bought (How it strikes me that he, so worthy of scorn, was never trash-talked by Abby; yet she, whom everyone regarded as an angel, was the constant target of his vitriol.)

On this vacation, I was happiest in solitude. I spent hours curled in a concave balcony facing the ocean. Its wrought-iron filigree offered the elegance Santa Clarita lacked. The faded yellow stucco walls welcomed writing. With a sketch pad (who bought it for me? Most probably Mom) I drew the shingled roofs that stretched out before me – imbrication, when I learned what that word meant, I remembered this moment – then I looked up to the quickly passing clouds: numbers, cars, cats and dogs in bowler hats walking on two legs.

After figure skating, I have never felt more content than when I was on that porch, imagining in that notebook, just dancing with time. Mom, I think, knew I was finding my element. It didn't make sense to her why this boy would want to curl up on a patio and pass his hours swirling a pen around in a notebook, but she did her best to understand. She told me, more than once, that one of her regrets in raising me was that she didn't encourage this creative side more. But coming from a tribe that never went to museums, that couldn't imagine the concept of musical theater or any non-transactional form of labor, there wasn't much she could do to raise an artistically inclined, fey child. Skating was her gift to me. Its figurations of lines on the blank page, recording in gossamer the flashing actions that once were so marvelous and *there*. The beauty and sadness of skating mirrors writing.

For all our years together, she'd remember those moments of spotting me "doodling" on the motel patio. She encouraged the self-expression, even if its form was foreign to her. It's more than my father could do. He wanted me in his own image — constantly sociable and adventurous to prove his worth. He wanted me outdoors, roughhousing with the other boys. He feared what I was becoming, and was always eager to object. But Mom was different. Fear never cowed her love. She didn't know precisely how I'd turn out, or what I'd choose in life, but she was faithful that she'd be there.

And she was. She read every issue of the university newspaper once I started as a contributor. She saved every single issue of *The Anchorage Press* once I was a culture reporter, going so far as to write my boss an effusive letter of praise, something to the effect of *Matt Caprioli makes things come alive!* "You have quite the fan…" he said, forwarding the email. I was too embarrassed to laugh it off, tell him that that person with a different last name was actually my mother. Instead, I scolded her for this intrusion into my personal life (even if it was a public newspaper). She apologized with no defense, saying she'd never do it again.

Now, I think, Good God: my greatest supporter in life, the woman who wanted to cheer me on in any and all ways possible — how could I cut her down?

A week before she passed, I told her I was to be published in *Chicken Soup for the Soul.* "Really?" she said weakly, her eyes surprised. Chicken Soup was a big deal for us. She bought me *Chicken Soup for the Teenage Soul* when I was 13. I bought her one for Mother's Day a year later. We went back and forth until I discovered Sartre and abandoned the series.

"Yeah Mom." I told her brightly. "I'm in."

"Ah, Mazing," she breathed, too weak to celebrate, annoyed with herself for being incapable of showing more enthusiasm; disappointed, too, perhaps, that she wouldn't live long enough to see it published.

I would like to write in a happier key. For now, let it suffice to say that she nurtured my greatest gift: writing.

CHAPTER 25

Sun

I suppose I must describe our final drive.

Abby last drove a few weeks before her death. To a doctor's appointment.

She was having a bad day, which for most people in her situation would be a good day. She didn't complain; she just wasn't her chipper self. She was like some of the dour cancer patients we had met around the infusion chair circuit, months and months ago, souls further along in their treatment; we couldn't entirely relate to them with their stereotyped movements, their thistle hair and battered mien. Mom's hair had thinned, (though with chemo stopped, some of the natural color was growing back). But I couldn't see her as a cancer patient, couldn't acknowledge the emaciation taking over, the waxen tawny in her skin that appeared at times in her eyes as splattered yellow paint. "I don't want this to define me," she told me. And further along, "I'm tired of being sick all the time."

Cancer is an unimaginable disease for all, save for those whose lives end in such pain. People disassociate entirely from their foundations, the very essence of "me" severed.

A couple of months after October 3rd, 2017, I walked out of a movie, "Film Stars Don't Die in Liverpool." It showed a woman dying of cancer, cared in part and ineptly by her lover and his family. It mirrored too closely my last days with Mom. That reflection of my experience was too much, even as I was capable of bearing the lived ordeal. Now, when I see pictures of Abby toward the end, my heart collapses. She was so clearly sick, fragile, off-color; her once lush hair wrecked to dehydrated, brittle strands. But in each moment, I never conceived of her as a cancer victim. I did not view her as "having" cancer. I always thought of her, inalterably, as Mom. Even when I approached her coffin. With each step closer, I sank further into the ground. My mouth broke out in horror at the first glimpse. They'd done a good job fixing her up, but the severely creased lines along her jaws, in a face that was always smiling, broke me. I approached further, using the pews as a crutch, one hand at a time, closer, then closer, until I was at the edge of the blue iron coffin.

"Oh Mom," I told her body. "This is fucking freaky," I said in a whisper, with a broken laugh. "You never liked this part of funerals, did you?" I chuckled in despair, a sort of swallowing, wallowing sound. "Remember that scene, what was it, *The Fighting Temptations?* Someone leans over and whispers — wake up! wake up!" I laughed. "That was good. We had a good time together now. Didn't we?"

This wasn't her. Yet a part of me accepted this corpse as Abby. I didn't touch her. I imagined the cold, the ice that had encased her for days; the memory of that cold would shadow too much joy.

But I'm not telling you of our last drive.

When I made it clear I'd pay for her housing, food, and transport, I said this was a new phase in her life. "This is like a new part-time job for you," I said happily over the phone, knowing that after her string of failed jobs in New York, she was looking for more steady employment in Alaska. (I cringe now at how unaware I was – and am – of the scars and terrors of cancer. The horror of a life rewritten. How blithely I proclaimed that her old life was over; that this new atrocity was to take over as top priority). "Use your energy to get better. Don't worry about money." Could I more cruelly have removed her from the state of ordinary affairs; did I have to be so confident that such withdrawal from daily life was in her best interest?

But I can't blame myself; this is to take more credit than my actions deserve. It's cancer to blame for her illness — a cruel, exacting reality. When Abby insisted on driving in the middle of September, that day that appeared to be "bad," she was not railing against my usurpation of her daily independence, so much as the disease. Fate. Her weakening body. For a woman who craved freedom and mobility above all else, the diagnosis was hell.

In the middle of August, she opened a letter to me with:

Dear Matthew,

These 'dog tags' came into my possession at a time in my life when I was young (22), physically strong (in good shape), and finally, I could support myself.

That now, nearing the end of 54, she could not support herself in any way, was just about intolerable. Perhaps sensing this rage against helplessness, I let her drive.

She drove slowly, and without incident. Her mood lifted. She grinned in accomplishment once she parked us safely in the garage off C Street. Perhaps she felt like a NASCAR victor as we huddled and hobbled together toward the elevator. The oncologist, far kinder than any of the professionals we had worked with previously, infused her port with a sodium-based solution. "Her marker levels aren't good," he told me. I told him she didn't want to hear specific numbers anymore.

Abby insisted on driving back, too.

"You're not too tired?"

"No, I can drive."

"I'd rather drive. Give you a break."

"Thank you Matthew, but I am totally fine to drive."

We moved slowly down the parking garage, lazy as a stuffed whale, looping around and around until we met Northern Lights Boulevard. She didn't see a car coming up fast. Or rather, she did see it, but her reflexes were slower now, so slow as to be completely apart from the woman in the Marines who won medals for shooting moving targets. She stopped just inches from the tiny car blazing by. We exclaimed Oh my god! (my version carried a *fucking*).

"Just pull over in the Key Bank lobby," I told her. "I can drive us home."

Her insistence was gone. The evidence was overwhelming. She could not endanger her son like this. She couldn't drive anymore.

I think of the artist Robert Rauschenberg after a stroke disabled his right hand. "Arne," he turned to a friend, "I have lost so much."

On Victoria's penultimate day on earth, Abby had annoyed her siblings by suggesting they take Victoria out for one more spin in a car.

"Are you crazy?" The eldest asked. "She's hardly conscious. She can hardly move. How will we get her in the car? Who's going to carry her?"

"What," Abby replied in mock-shock. "She's still breathing. She knows what's going on. Just a few blocks around the neighborhood. She'd love it."

But Abby was outvoted. Victoria stayed put, passing the next morning.

"It was actually peaceful," Abby told me more than once, almost insistently. "You could just feel her leave the room. I had gone in there to tell her we were going across the street for coffee. Her one eye was really big, wide open. Like she was telling me to stay. I called for Jeremiah and Rhoda to come in. They did. We all laid hands on her. Then she took a deep breath in, then an extra-long exhale. And Matthew, it was beautiful, really. You could feel her leave the room. And, sad as we were, you know, it was okay."

This is all to say that Abby, who loved her mother deeply, thought driving was one of the greatest gifts you could give someone. Driving and all it represented — freedom, possibility, connection, autonomy, a turning view of the beautiful world.

I tried to honor this love. I tried. But I didn't hold her in the moments after she stopped breathing. I couldn't bring myself to close her eyes, which had filled entirely with a black toxin; I couldn't bring myself to take her pulse, though I held her hand.

She headed out at 5pm on a Tuesday to "Amazing Grace."

I wonder if that song she'd heard all her life gave her comfort and strength. And strength, perhaps, to give herself over — to jump into whatever was coming next, all that was pulling her away from this life — to finally (finally) let go.

Our last drive: seven days before her heart stopped, the kind oncologist told me, "The truth is she's dying." A pause. "I recommend hospice."

I asked him how long. He sucked his teeth. The final prognosis was the hardest part of his job.

"It's hard to say. I believe about 2 to 3 months. It could be as long as six months. It could be a few weeks. But I do think it's important to get hospice paperwork started. The last thing you want is a rushed arrangement with hospice. I've seen that with so many families."

The literal deadline churned me into numbness. Everything I thought I knew was not so. My mother would not live forever, no matter how many times I successfully bounced a balloon on my head, or what new treatments I found in New York and Canada.

"She's against hospice," I told him. "She thinks it means we're giving up on her."

His look held empathy and patience.

"Go talk to her."

Mom had another flush of sodium-water through her port. She was weak, skeletal, but she remained upbeat, her eyes bright, her smile steady, bright lipstick applied. The nurses loved her. Abby remembered their kids' names and grades. She remembered how all of them got to Alaska.

"What did the good doc say," she asked me with a smile from the chair.

How would I tell the truth, but tell it slant? I knew the numbers. The forecasts. The options considered and striked out. I smiled at her. Her beauty and brightness were nearly enough to forget the pain.

"Let's go for a ride."

In good cheer, we had said bye to all the nurses. We acted as if we were leaving the salon. And considering how the nurses let me sit in the infusion chair next to Mom, both of our legs propped high, our eyes out to the mountains as mechanical pulses massaged our backs, a spa was easy to imagine.

The elevator took us to the top of the parking garage. I had gotten into the habit of parking Matey on the roof, with the phenomenal view of the mountains to the north, the cityscape to the south. We huddled together and walked. Her body had become so small, frail. Her movements were slow, hesitant.

Leaving the parking garage, I turned Matey north on Benson Boulevard.

"Let's have some fun," I calmly proclaimed to Mom.

She beamed, looking at the mountains on this impossibly clear day. "Let's."

The first stop was Burger King. I would get all our favorites — vanilla smoothies, chicken fingers, the famous French fries with extra salt. It was near Alaska Club North, one of two indoor tennis courts. In high school, I'd cross town on the bus for two hours from the south side to the north just to play tennis against a wall, the ball machine, or the stray team member who happened to be around. Playing tennis in California would have been, of course, easier, what with the nearby courts, constant sunshine, and my father's readiness to pay for private lessons, so long as I treated tennis as a ladder for social mobility. But I'd rather take all the shit I experienced growing up in Alaska, always in the context of love, than the comfort of life in SoCal, where a nourishing love did not exist. I'd rather take Mom sick and ghastly, than act like my sister, who didn't even try to help her through the pain, who didn't acknowledge that this all was real and finite.

And yet, I could not tell Abby what the doctor said. I quietly bemoaned why this burden – to tell my mother she soon would die – was placed on me. I could not figure out how to tell her.

So we drove. Next: a Best Buy on the edge of town. I wanted to reenact our famous road trip from 2009, after I had completed a year of college and we found a new cordiality and intimacy as adults; when we listened to Lady Gaga, Santigold, and The Yeah Yeah Yeahs. Walking briskly through the music section of the Tikahtnu Center, I bought three

CDs. That I can only easily recall one — Beyoncé's "Lemonade" — makes me think that some moments are truly singular. Apexes do exist. As do epochs. Time is unrepeatable. Even the most resplendent ending is brutal in its limits.

The day was brilliant; the sunshine was constant. We breezed up north on the Glenn Highway. I felt ebullient — vaguely as if we were escaping the disease.

Around Peter's Creek, just minutes into neighboring Eagle River, Mom asked me to pull over.

"I'm sorry," she whispered. "I'm not feeling well."

I pulled over at the next stop. Down the road was where we had a Thanksgiving dinner with the Jews for Jesus, a wacky bunch, friends primarily of Grandma. After a violently homophobic prayer at the table by the pastor/rabbi, I told Mom I had something to tell her. I was 16. She was 44.

"I think I'm gay."

I cried in shame. She patted my knees, looked at me tenderly.

"Well, Matthew. Thank you for telling me. I didn't know you felt that way. I want you to know I still love you very much. You understand that?" And with that, the leaden secret lifted. For the first time in years, I could breathe freely.

She opened the door to Matey. I heard her retch up the vanilla shake. I patted her back, the nubs of her spine. I rubbed her shoulder. "It's okay," I said in a lie-coo. "It's okay. Get it out." I looked at the beauty of fall leaves down St. Peter's Road.

How had we come to this?

When she sounded done, had caught her breath once more, I handed her tissues.

"I'm sorry, Matthew." I could taste the acrid smell.

I suddenly remembered a young woman named Kat. I gave her a ride shortly after meeting Jack, the first guy I fell in love with. He was in the closet at 21. She was a former girlfriend of his, someone he dated in high school when he was known as a cocky artist-jock. Kat was too drunk and eager to regain Jack that she didn't realize he and I were staring at each other the entire night.

She needed a ride home from the bar, and wanting to impress Jack with my new car – the Matrix that Mom insisted on calling Matey – I offered to drive her home. Several blocks from the bar, she started to vomit small chunks. I rolled down the window.

"Out of the window please out of the window," I commanded, pushing her toward the window. "This car is brand new."

Her head dropped to her knees, where she vomited in full earnestness. "Oh c'mon" I cried to her blacked-out form. I slowed to 10 mph, coasting down the empty fareway of Avenue C at 3am. I reached across her to open the passenger door. Noting her seat belt fastened, I pushed her out of the car. Her mouth left trails of vomit along the snowy roads. The full stank didn't leave Matey for half a year.

I thought of telling Abby this anecdote after she threw up. "See, you're in worse shape than Kat, but your manners are still so much better! You're too polite to even vomit in the car." No doubt, she would have laughed. But I couldn't bring myself to say anything. I looked away as she vomited and bit my lip.

We drove home in a rare silence, both focused only on what lay immediately ahead. There was no place else to go beyond our makeshift home in South Anchorage. Matey took us there. But I was not quite ready to turn in. The day was still beautiful. I suggested we get some sun before heading home. The nearest lakes we loved were too far. Mom was getting tired, more than she was letting on. I parked us in an empty lot near a sizeable stone church. We faced east, toward the sun. We were to have a gentle, happy, sunny picnic, like so many times before.

Gently, she asked, "Would you like to tell me what the doctor said?"

I looked at her. She was corralling bravery. Ready as ever.

"It doesn't look good," I said, not meeting her face. "He thinks we should prepare..." I couldn't say it. Hospice. Your death. I looked at her. I was in pain. That much was clear. She was taking on the role of comforter. As she always did (and in my memory, does). She reached for my hand. I clasped her hand.

I cinched my eyes shut, but tears came down.

"If I lose you," I managed to say. "I will be devastated." No other words came through.

She patted my hand. A sadness, but a hope, too. A will to be of good cheer, to have faith.

"Oh, Matthew," she said. "I still have hope. I still believe one of these new therapies will work."

I didn't snap at her. I didn't flinch at this. A part of me thought her beliefs were juvenile or killing her. I didn't agree with them, but there was something about her conviction, her constancy in believing, almost for the sake of belief, that crystalized for me why she was good.

I suggested we lean our seats all the way back. She agreed. I opened the sunroof. We lay under the sun, holding hands. Parked. In Alaska. Near a church. Listening to our breath. Not knowing where to go or what would happen next. Feeling not luck, but comfort. The quiet happiness of being together.

CHAPTER 26

5pm

In 24 hours, Mom would be near mute and hopelessly weak. But that Thursday afternoon, skeletal as she had become, she seemed far from death. She applied her reddest shade of lipstick. She smiled cheerfully, full of magnanimity, as she moved slowly from her double-mattress bed to a green velour chair in the living room. A good half hour before schedule, she was ready for her appointment with the magnificently named Donna Bacon.

Donna was about her age, early 50s. Her blonde bob and steady-but-never-uncontrolled smile suggested she was one for fun, but hardly a dainty hack therapist who would skirt the difficult truth. She was a "palliative care" coordinator with Veterans Affairs, which is to say she helped people prepare themselves for dying.

She bonded quickly with Abby during their weekly sessions in the months before I moved up there. A couple of weeks after this final session, Donna attended the funeral. "I didn't know Abby for long," she told me. "But I felt very close to her. In other circumstances, I would have liked to be her friend."

That Thursday session was to be the first of several group sessions: me, Mom, and Donna. I still had trouble accepting the doctor's prognosis, and I was hoping to have Donna help me convey (and absorb) the magnitude of what was to come.

She entered our one-bedroom apartment, decorated all homey with plaques of horses, Bible verses, and posters of Alaska, doused in a rose light from several pink lamp shades. We offered Donna a taller foldout chair meant for the outdoors. I sat on the air mattress. We were thus in a circle of various heights: Donna the highest, Abby in the middle, me at the bottom.

Donna asked Abby how she was doing, talked about the growing flowers she had seen on the drive over here. Abby, now in sunken thinness, listened with rapture. The smallest detail, if conveyed by someone she loved, was to Abby the greatest jewel. She looked up at Donna with a great smile, her shoulders back, spine straight — sociable as ever. How skillfully she hid her pain.

We exchanged a few more pleasantries, then Donna came out with the truth. "You don't look so good, Abby."

"Oh Donna well." Abby wasn't entirely sure how to respond. She had on her best lipstick. She had found energy to apply mascara. "I feel fine."

"You're not just telling us that?"

Abby's smile showed a deep dimple on the right cheek. "You know," she turned her head toward Donna, as if they both were part of a warm joke. "I'm not one to pull your leg." She referred to some experimental trials her oncologist was arranging. "He's such a good man," Abby repeated. "He really cares for his patients."

Donna nodded solemnly.

"I still have hope I'm gonna beat this thing," Abby said. Her tone was all conviction, but her voice was reedier, like she was breathing at too high an altitude.

Donna was too smart to show much sadness. "Alright then," She clasped her hands softly. "Shall we begin?"

I have a phrase now for my father, or rather the impulse that subsumed much of his life.

Toxic masculinity.

A descendent of fascism, toxic masculinity is what I, now 30, see so clearly was ailing my father.

Toxic masculinity has become tossed around so often its meaning is obscured. Often it's set off like a smoke bomb; in the clearing, people can see whatever they wish. The phrase itself can get people nodding their heads or leaving a table before they pass a few seconds in contemplating its application. For me, I hesitate to use it toward my father because it captures his situation so well that I wish it weren't the case. At times, I wish I was one of those blithe people who scoff at the phrase *toxic masculinity* and disdain "libtard" conceptions like *safe spaces* and *microaggressions*. At times, I've envied those blunted psyches who keep well-thought truth at an abstract, toothless distance.

Decades later, it can be easy to forget how terrorized I was of my father. I called in "sick" one day from school when I was eight. My mother knew about these absences; we both knew it was better not to tell my father, who'd say that toughing it out was part of real life. While I was greedily watching daytime talk shows on the living room TV, Dad unexpectedly came home. Instead of saying I was sick and pretending to cough, I jumped behind the couch, where I hid from him for the next three hours.

At 12, I watched some scary movie about a home robbery. That night, I locked my windows and placed traps around my room, including several books around my bed for an intruder to trip on, and a dirty clothes basket behind the door to delay the attack. My dad came in late that night to my room for some reason. Seeing that a hamper of dirty clothes was blocking the door triggered him. The smallest of surprise obstacles was, for him, the gravest personal assault; the world was a giant fuck-you unless you fucked it first. He was eager to show, by any force necessary, that he would not tolerate any form of insubordination. I was drifting to sleep one moment, then the next, opened my eyes to see my father raising the basket of laundry above his head. "What the fuck is this?" he roared. He threw it hard as he could against the wall.

There are hundreds of other examples like this, to the point that my memory is almost entirely dark from the ages of 10 to 13. Except for when visiting Mom, I was incorrigibly silent. I grew numb. Days were indistinguishable. There was nothing to look forward to, nothing to record or remember. My father spent his weekends with a new girlfriend around Pasadena, and my half-sister spent the evening, if not the night, with friends. I did not think it odd to spend weekends alone until Mom pointed it out to me. I was content enough playing "Grand Theft Auto" and "Crash Bandicoot."

My existence became one where I did not think. Maya Angelou once wrote, *The intensity with which young people live demands that they "blank out" as often as possible.* My voided memory under a tyrannical father approached this "blanking out," this near annihilation.

As a college student, I responded to a study about suicide. I called a number, answered five questions, and was informed that I did not qualify for the study that would lead to a $50 gift card. "We're looking for people who thought about self-harm," the graduate student kindly told me, "but did not actually go through with any self-harm."

I wanted to laugh. For some reason, I had answered yes to the inflicting self-harm. "You know the melodramatic stuff," I had lied. "Like surface cuts on the wrist."

I had attempted to lie my way into a psychology study. Surely, I reasoned, it was more probable for a study on suicide to be concerned with the most dramatic cases, so I invented some stakes and shallow knife wounds.

I didn't think clearly as to why I was lying; I was surprised that I felt the need to lie, but perhaps a part of me wanted to talk about suicide, including my own brushes with it. The gift card would have bought a nice new beanie, but the main prospect was for someone to look at my experience objectively, perhaps compassionately.

It humors me nearly into silence that I was exactly the sort of participant this study wanted, yet my own manipulative nature, helped perhaps by stereotypes on suicide, led me away from reality. The truth was that I had tapped a butcher knife along the downward slant of my wrist's largest vein. The truth was that I daydreamed about running into traffic, or jumping from one of the many cliffs I passed by on the way to school. The truth was that I tied bedsheets several times around a banister, then my neck. The truth was that I read news about a 14-year-old gay kid killing himself, and I thought about the peace he must have found with all of this just over.

But I never hurt myself.

I wanted to be honest as I could with Abby. I wanted to tell her how much I truly loved her, how sorry I was for all the times I failed. In asking myself why I never self-harmed, the answer alighted on me as clearly as a once tricky math problem.

Donna asked if I had anything to say. Abby turned to me pleasantly as if this was just a tea time check in with friends. I told her the truth.

"When I was down in California, I was not happy. You knew that. I mean, I have never been that depressed. That was the lowest point of my life, and every day I woke up just without any will. I had no friends. My dad was incredibly domineering. I was in the closet, and I didn't know what to do about it. I really didn't want to live."

I told them about the rougher encounters with Dad. In the kitchen when he was screaming at me to be more of a man, to make friends already, and "stop being such a goddamn pathetic pussy." I left the kitchen table to cry alone in my room. "Get back here and sit down," he yelled. I continued walking away. He sprang up from the chair and lurched at me. I ran toward the kitchen. He ran after me. I crouched beneath the kitchen island. Either way he came at me, I'd go the opposite.

"Come out and face me like a fucking man," he shouted.

Trapped, I finally screamed, "Please leave me alone!" A piercing sharpness entered my abdomen. All the mental pain and stress of that moment compacted in my belly, and I keeled over, eventually falling to my knees. All the mourning I had within me was released into a stream of guttural sobs. I slid further along the floor.

"Fine," I heard my father. His voice was dark, low, full of spite. "If you want to be alone, suit yourself."

He left. I recovered breathing on the ground. He didn't lay a finger on me, yet I had never felt so powerfully attacked.

"You saved my life," I finally tell Mom. "I don't think I'm being inaccurate or overly dramatic when I say that. When I lived with Dad, that was just a dark time. I honestly feel that it was a 50-50 chance that one day, if I kept living with Dad, it all would get to be too much, and I wouldn't be here today. I honestly believe that is true. I just wanted you to know that, and to thank you."

I was looking at the ceiling for most of this time to keep my thoughts straight. When I looked at Mom, her fragile mouth was open, confused and perhaps shocked by this; she knew I was unhappy, but not suicidal. At times, I wonder if I should have kept this intense episode secret; she didn't need the stress of such histories interfering with her last days. But I wanted her to know, as viscerally as I did, that her life was of great worth; that she allowed other people to live.

When I turned to Donna, a diamond tear was in the middle of her cheek. She realized it once I looked at her, and quickly wiped it away. She resumed a professional stature. I have wondered if I was performing for Donna. That I needed her as a witness to our story, and in my need for an audience, I manipulated the facts, as I did for that psychology study. But I didn't manipulate anything in that final session. Donna enabled the truth to come out. I could not identify, let alone carry, the velocity of my obligation and gratitude for Mom without someone as strong as Donna. She helped me tell Mom how much she mattered.

We all hugged goodbye, Mom staying in her chair. Donna was going to New Orleans for the week, but said she'd see us all as soon as she got back.

Once the door shut, Mom smiled at me. She was exhausted, yet lighter, somehow. She took a long nap in the chair. I applied for jobs, careful to type quietly. I felt relieved and calm, like I had finally acted in a manner that − difficult as it was − I would not regret.

The last 12 hours of her life were by turns miraculous and harrowing. Around 4am or 5am, I heard Abby moaning. The hospital had loaded her up on meds when she left, and their potency was diminishing. Jeremy was sleeping at her side, giving her a low dose of morphine every hour. It dissolved through her cheek to instantly enter her bloodstream. I told myself he could take care of her, and kept my delirious ass in bed, even as the moans grew louder.

She was still moaning when I got up to check on her around 7am. By then, the sun was out enough for me to see her eyes, bulging with pain.

I did not wait. I did not ask Jeremy if he was keeping up with the dosage. I did not call the hospice nurse to be put on hold. I grabbed the morphine and filled two vials. I would become intimate with the gentle clack of plastic against her beautiful teeth. The moaning stopped almost immediately.

A hospice nurse came at 9am. We had only met him once before yesterday. He looked over the discharge paperwork before confirming that we could give her a higher dosage. "In fact, this is really on the low side for someone in her state."

I don't think I will ever forgive myself for allowing her to go through hours of unimaginable pain. Nor will I forgive the apathetic professionals I had called to confirm dosages, who told me to just stick with the discharge papers until a nurse arrived for a check-up.

Her body was relaxed for the next two hours. By 11am, she was approaching her last hour of lucidity. A slick-black toxin was starting to fill her eyes. It appeared first in her right eye; her head was facing to the right, toward the patio window filling with light. A blot of ink was dappling the white of her eye here and there, the ink insidiously expanding. Then more terrible marks, definitive as brushstrokes, covered her eyes. It had never been so implacable: I was losing my mother.

Only weeks later would I be brave enough to mentally articulate her own horror: she was losing her life. Her son. Her husband. She was 54; 55 in a month. She had a daughter whose wedding she wanted to see. A son whose future she was betting on. She had just completed a master's degree. She was ready to turn her life around. She had so much to live for. She did not want to die.

When I saw the toxins taking over her eyes, how much worse it must have been to live it. I imagine it is a drowning of the soul, the gradual loss of vision, even as one forces the eyes to grow wider and wider, one is incapable, and the walls keep closing in, or perhaps the picture is scratched beyond reckoning, scratches compounding.

She knew that she was going blind. She knew that she could no longer speak, not even raise a finger to signal she'd heard us say *Love you*. Her eyes would be her final goodbye. She knew this.

I leaned over the bulky hospice bed, gazing into her eyes, forcing my vision to hold steady, even as horror was taking over my mother. I am proud of myself for not looking away, and I believe that she was too. As the first spot of black dotted her left eye, she looked at me with all her force of being.

That look was her goodbye. It carried with it every good wish for me, every moment we shared together, every drive, every hug, every wish, ever torment, every dream and every prayer. We confided in each other; we loved each other; we hated and failed each other. We were always there and always would be there. That look was full of the utmost compassion. The utmost blessing. It was our entire relationship condensed into a few immaculate moments. It was *Sorry I have to go*. It was *God bless you and keep you my son*. It was *What a ride, my life; what joy*. It was *I don't want to go*. It was *I am ready to*.

That look was a grace as absolute and infinite as the force that lifted our Mustang up a mountain, despite the weather that could have killed us.

Then her eyes were no more, and her breathing was sharper. Then I sang to her. Then Adam appeared, rushing from New York to say goodbye to this woman he loved. Then Jeremy in his country twang: "Honey, it looks like our Maker is calling you home. I sure do love you. You're always going to be with me here, okay. In my heart. And I'll be seeing you." Then he cried softly in the corner. Then *Amazing Grace* by Darlene Zschech came on. Then she inhaled one time.

And did not exhale.

Just like that.

At 5pm.

Like she was clocking out.

I wanted to howl. But there were neighbors around. And Jeremy and Adam. I didn't want my grief to scare them. I didn't want Mom to leave this world with the sound of wailing.

I ran to the bedroom that had been her own for a year. I went to the open closet and clutched her dresses and sweaters hanging up. I buried my face into the soft dresses – red and mauve and white – I opened my mouth wide as possible, furling it into impossible expressions that I would learn is the torn face of absolute grief. I cried and cried. I cried every day. I would come to know that there would never be enough tears.

Part Three

...I've been thinking: This is what the living do. And
      yesterday, hurrying along those
wobbly bricks in the Cambridge sidewalk, spilling my
      coffee down my wrist and sleeve,

I thought it again, and again later, when buying a hairbrush:
      This is it.
Parking. Slamming the car door shut in the cold. What you
      called *that yearning.*

What you finally gave up. We want the spring to come and
      the winter to pass. We want
whoever to call or not call, a letter, a kiss—we want more
      and more and then more of it.

But there are moments, walking, when I catch a glimpse of
      myself in the window glass,
say, the window of the corner video store, and I'm gripped
      by a cherishing so deep

for my own blowing hair, chapped face, and unbuttoned
      coat that I'm speechless:
I am living. I remember you.

                    —Marie Howe, "What the Living Do"

CHAPTER 27

The Mountain

It's July 18th, 2020.

It will be three years in October.

What a hoot Mom has missed. I wonder what she would think of Covid-19, the spectacular rise of AOC, the terrorist attack at an Ariana Grande concert, my purchase of a fancy keyboard that I've named Eleanor, the murder of George Floyd, my "adult" apartment in Queens, my project on Jasper Johns and Robert Rauschenberg. How much would she have laughed and cried at "Ladybird," "Girls Trip," "Second Act," "Good Boys," "Hustlers," "Book Smart." I wonder how she would develop beyond her conservative roots. Her compassion and understanding would eventually come to support Black Lives Matter; I believe she would grow out of reactionary beliefs of "reverse racism" to see the problem with "Blue Lives Matter." She couldn't bring herself to vote for Hillary, would probably feel uncomfortable around Elizabeth Warren and Bernie Sanders, but I could see her voting for Joe Biden in 2020, the first vote she'd have cast for a Democrat. Just as she would want to see me marry and care for her grandchildren, so would I like to watch her grow into the mind she was developing, the sort of person she always wanted to be.

Each year, on the day of her death, October 3rd, I spend most of the day volunteering. Her passing should bring about something positive. I donate clothes and electronics to women's shelters, write a check to the Syrian Refuge

Project, donate to the Colon Cancer Alliance and The V Foundation. In every action I remember Abby's chief motivation: to help others.

On her birthday, November 20th, I cook a large meal and celebrate her life with friends. Most of them in New York never knew Abby, and she never knew them, but I know she'd enjoy hearing from them: our petty bosses, our unique hair removal remedies, run-ins with exes on the Q train, our thoughts on the latest fiction bestseller. Abby loved people. She loved the human body, hence her studying biology and keeping two large posters of the skeletal and muscular system in all of her passing rooms in Alaska. She loved hearing people's thoughts, hence her passionate inquiry of strangers, her love of psychology and constant desire to be of service. With each meal I cook on her birthday, I forward the love she showed to everyone.

I have gone from an embittered freelance writer to an editor in financial consulting to becoming a faculty member in the English department of Lehman College. Victoria always told me "Respect your teachers. They work so hard and they care for you." Abby called me "Professor Matthew" after my first year of college.

At 30, I've finally found a vocation that does not feel like work. A dream job, truly. How thrilled they'd be for me. I can picture Abby jumping up and down at the news, ecstatic beyond belief, as she was when I read my college acceptance letter, or each time she spotted me walking toward her at the airport.

About a year after her death, I started a Google Doc, "All I'd Share with You." It ran from November 15, 2018 to August 19, 2019. There's Willie Nelson's cover of "Unchained Melody." One link is to *The Anchorage Daily News'* reporting on "Wild Ice," a documentary on backcountry skiing — skaters moving fast on open ice around Alaska. The word *Guava* appears without explanation. A picture I took from December 1, 2019, of the sun rising along the East River. The "Active Wear" parody video. "Duele el Corazón" by Enrique Iglesias, as well as "Arr. Kreisler: Song without Words, op. 62 No. 1 (arr. for Violin and Piano)" by Vilde Frang and José Gallardo. I have pictures of the new Whitney location to send her; newspaper clips on "stereotype threat," the topic of her master's thesis; a parody of Camilla Cabello's "Havana" with a rubber chicken. Dave Barry's article on finally getting a colonoscopy. The Irena Sendler Project. Diana Damrau singing Mozart's "Queen of the Night" aria, the top YouTube comment being, "Honestly if i had a voice like that, I'd yell at my kids the same way too."

There are other links to YouTube that show, "This video is no longer available because the YouTube account associated with this video has been terminated." There are empty bullet points where I meant to type something.

I smile.

What was I trying to share with her? What is lost when the items we wish to ferry fail to meet the loved one? After a while, you have to smile because none of it matters. All the things I'd share with you — she already knew what they were. That's why I planned to send them her way. She already loved them all.

I quickly sold the Toyota Matrix to pay off the accumulated debt of the funeral, plane tickets, rent for the one-bedroom in South Anchorage. I regretted selling Matey almost instantly. A year later, I offered to buy the car back from the seller. No response. I can't blame her. Adam and I were in a rush to return to New York and sold it for a bargain.

The last piece of property that binds Victoria, Abby, and myself together is the house on Lazy Mountain. In trying to move it to my name, I learned that the house is in fact considered a cabin, and that it was never probably recorded under my family's name. It belongs, on paper, to a dead man who has held the deed since 1992. An uncle of mine paid $8,000 for it in 1998, all for nil, it would seem. To make my family's ownership of the house real will cost over $7,000 in legal fees. Some have told me to let the property pass; lord knows *the shredders* are still up there, and the cabin will likely need to be razed. Yet I've come to understand that I need to fight for this land. I need to fight for my loved ones.

I plan to keep that land outside of Palmer. I will pull the weeds, re-paint the walls, maybe spend thousands for some indoor plumbing. I will grow that house to welcome in others. When I visit Mom, I will stay up there. When I have kids, we can vacation there for the summer. On the land itself, they'll feel glimpses of Abigail Ruth Frye, and her mother, Emma Castillo. I'll tell them these stories and more as we drive up the mountain together.

Acknowledgments

Innumerable people have supported my love for writing. Specifically for *One Headlight*, I want to thank Stacey Engels, H'Rina DeTroy, and Jen Lue for commenting on early drafts of this memoir. Your insight, generosity, and fabulous souls continually inspire me, and I am honored to count you as friends.

Joe Okonkwo also read my first attempt at memoir, and his detailed, trenchant feedback was an immense buoy during a time of great uncertainty.

The Hunter College MFA program was life-changing, and I want to thank my beautiful cohort, 2015-2017.

When I interned at *The Paris Review*, some of the first people I showed any creative writing to were Catherine Carberry, Lynette Lee, Michael Maier, Lawrence Freedman, and Joseph Wolin. That these brilliant people encouraged me to continue writing meant everything, and I doubt I would have had the confidence to apply to an MFA program without their support.

I was fortunate to have courageous and inspiring English teachers at A.J. Dimond High and at The University of Alaska, Anchorage. Susan Derrera, Suzanne Forster, and Rob Crosman each gave me permission to love literature and changed my life. Thank you.

My Alaska Texting Girl Crew: Amy Kirkham, Becca Hartley, and Brittany Bennett, thank you for being as ridiculous and lovely as I am. My bro book club, Rakin Azfar & Piotr Pillardy, thank you for the weekly inspiration while writing

One Headlight. Cinderblock People – Emily, Pat & Otis – the Bue Herons, especially Sara Qureshi and Tiffany Cordero, my NYC & Clarkie friends — I love you.

Thank you City University of New York and my Lehman College family for your belief in me. Thank you to the remarkable editors, readers, and writers at Cirque, a community I have admired from afar since stocking *Cirque* in UAA's bookstore over a decade ago.

Adam, whom Abby and Victoria adored, I don't know what I did in the past life to deserve you, and as annoying as your perfectionism can be, I thank my stars each day for you and your family that has welcomed me with open arms.

To the man I call Jeremy, as well as Michelle Dronge, Sarah Hernandez, Terri Barnum, Donna Bacon, and Marcia Weare — thank you.

None of this would have happened without my grandmother and mother; to Victoria and Abby, my deepest love, gratitude, and continual thanks.

About the Author

MATT CAPRIOLI is a queer Alaskan/NYC-based creative writer and Lecturer in the English Department of Lehman College, City University of New York. His creative and academic work explores subversion, sexuality, intimacy, and mixed-raced identity. His essays and fiction have appeared in *Epiphany*, *Breadcrumbs*, *Opossum Literary*, *Best Gay Stories 2017*, and *Newtown Literary*. As a journalist, he was a regular contributor to *Anchorage Press* and *The Red Hook Star-Revue*. He holds an MFA from Hunter College and is pursuing an MBA at Baruch College. Born in California in 1990, Caprioli now lives in Astoria, Queens with his partner, Adam.

About Cirque Press

Cirque Press grew out of *Cirque*, a literary journal that publishes the works of writers and artists from the North Pacific Rim, a region that reaches north from Oregon to the Yukon Territory, south through Alaska to Hawaii, and west to the Russian Far East.

Cirque Press is a partnership of Sandra Kleven, publisher, and Michael Burwell, editor. Ten years ago, we recognized that works of talented writers in the region were going unpublished, and the Press was launched to bring those works to fruition. We publish fiction, non-fiction, and poetry, and we seek to produce art that provides a deeper understanding about the region and its cultures. The writing of our authors is significant, personal, and strong.

Sandra Kleven – Michael Burwell
Publishers and Editors
www.cirquejournal.com

Books by Cirque Press

Apportioning the Light by Karen Tschannen (2018)

The Lure of Impermanence by Carey Taylor (2018)

Echolocation by Kristin Berger (2018)

Like Painted Kites & Collected Works by Clifton Bates (2019)

Athabaskan Fractal: Poems of the Far North by Karla Linn Merrifield (2019)

Holy Ghost Town by Tim Sherry (2019)

Drunk on Love: Twelve Stories to Savor Responsibly by Kerry Dean Feldman (2019)

Wide Open Eyes: Surfacing from Vietnam by Paul Kirk Haeder (2020)

Silty Water People by Vivian Faith Prescott (2020)

Life Revised by Leah Stenson (2020)

Oasis Earth: Planet in Peril by Rick Steiner (2020)

The Way to Gaamaak Cove by Doug Pope (2020)

Loggers Don't Make Love by Dave Rowan (2020)

The Dream That Is Childhood by Sandra Wassilie (2020)

Seward Soundboard by Sean Ulman (2020)

The Fox Boy by Gretchen Brinck (2021)

Lily Is Leaving: Poems by Leslie Ann Fried (2021)

One Headlight by Matt Caprioli (2021)

November Reconsidered by Marc Janssen (2021)

Someday I'll Miss This Place Too by Dan Branch (2021)

Out There In The Out There by Jerry McDonnell (2021)

Fish the Deep Water Hard by Eric Heyne (2021)

Miss Tami, Is Today Tomorrow? by Tami Phelps (2021)

CIRCLES Imprint

Lullaby for Bay Abe by Anne Chandonnet (2021)

Made in the USA
Middletown, DE
21 July 2021